DEDICATION

This book is dedicated to every job seeker. May you be strong, smart, and courageous in exploring life.

CONTENTS

1 WHO NEEDS THIS BOOK AND WHY

Choose a job you love, and you will never have to work a day in your life.

— *Anonymous*

This book is written for the readership who wants to find out about the best jobs in the United States. There are many ways to measure the quality of a job, and the measurement can be subjective. Indeed, depending on perspectives, a man's dream might be another man's nightmare.

In this book, instead of narrowly focusing on one criterion to measure jobs which some might agree and others might not, we examine multiple facets of job quality, including salary, job growth outlook, geographical distribution, and impact of education on job quality.

We base the analyses in this book not on subjective

opinions but rather on data that is of unmatched breadth and quality. The data was collected on 156 million jobs across 820 occupations by the U.S. government, newly released in May and October 2017.

If you are a fan of empirical data and insights derived from actual data, this book contains a lot for you to feast on. If you are new to data driven insights, this book serves as a great opportunity for you to open eyes to the vast amount of occupational insights revealed in this massive data from the most authoritative source.

With a focus on salary and job growth outlook, this book also analyzes the reasons behind astonishing disparities in salary and growth outlook across occupations that must be incorporated into one's career decisions.

To facilitate sound career choices, this book further teaches a ranking method for the reader to evaluate and compare available occupation options in a consistent and systematic way, toward the end of the book.

This method is straightforward and simple to implement; you can easily incorporate your own preferences and priorities to produce personalized job rankings. In other words, after reading this book, you will be able to compare and contrast your occupation choices through the ranking made by yourself.

This stands in sharp contrast to job rankings that are found in the media; there, the rankings are produced by some opaque algorithms that typically do not reflect your priorities in making occupation choices. The reason is simple: The journalists making the rankings in those newspaper or magazine articles do not know you, let alone your preferences or priorities.

This book is for anyone who is interested in finding out about the best jobs to make the best career decisions. For those who are new to the labor market, including college seniors, graduate school students, and high school students, this book provide you with vital information to help you make the right career choices.

For those who are needed to provide career counseling, for instance college and high school career counselors, and student parents and guardians, this book provides you with the most up to date occupational information to back up your advices and guidance.

For those who already have a job, there is invaluable information contained in this book for you to chew on, and can help you evaluate your current job against what else is out there.

Specifically, this book is for you if you fall into any of the following groups.

College and graduate school students who are thinking about next steps after graduation: Am I on the right track to a decent job after graduation that meets my career aspiration? I heard about recent college graduates who had the same major as mine; their got jobs but are not paid well at all. What level of pay should I expect for my major? I am graduating; should I find a job or pursue further education? What is the tradeoff?

High school students who feel the need to start thinking about career plans: This book offers comprehensive and reliable information about the best jobs in the U.S. It is in your best interest to take it into account in making smart career path decisions to ready yourself for the upcoming adulthood.

Parents and guardians of high school students who are helping their children make career plans: The information provided in this book enables the parents to provide effective guidance that your children need in making wise decisions that will have long lasting implications in the quality of your children's life.

Such decisions typically include whether to pursue a college education and if yes what major to study. If college is not in the plan that your children are making for the years after graduation, what professions would you recommend your children to pursue and why? This book provides a lot of clues to these questions.

High school career counselors who want to advise students and parents on career planning: With this book, you can confidently respond to the questions such as: What kinds of jobs are out there? Which jobs are the best in the country and why? What are the fastest growing jobs in the years to come? What jobs are endangered and should be avoided?

Current employees who cannot stop wondering about these questions: How does my job compare to others? Are there other jobs that can better meet my needs than my current one? Regardless of whether you just joined the workforce or are already an experienced employee, this book helps answer these burning questions and guides you to the right directions before it is too late to make changes.

Anyone else who are interested in being well informed about different kinds of jobs available out there in the U.S., the stunning disparities in the rewards the jobs bring to us, the fastest growing jobs, and the quickest disappearing jobs in the years to come.

If you are in any of these groups, keep on reading. This book is definitely for you.

Before we delve into all the details later in this book, we will touch upon the following topics in this introductory chapter:

Why choosing the right job is of huge importance?

Why should I read *this* book for guidance on selecting jobs?

What aspects of jobs does this book address?

The focus of this book is not on individual employment opportunities or positions, but rather on occupations. When we say jobs in this book, we mean occupations or professions. The reader should treat jobs, occupations and professions interchangeably in this book.

The only exception is when we say that the data on which this book is based on covers 156 million jobs, we mean 156 million positions. Obviously, there are not 156 million different occupations in this world. Not even close. The data covers 156 million positions across 820 occupations.

How Important Is Choosing an Occupation

Most of us will have to take a job, sooner or later in our life, to bring in income to support ourselves and our families. Of course, some of us are fortunate enough to be born into a blue blood or otherwise rich family, and therefore expect to inherit a good deal of fortune.

In these lucky cases, we might not need to worry about landing a decent job, although we might still want one for fun or for other purposes, but not for the purposes of supporting ourselves.

For the rest of us, having a good job is a must in order to lead a comfortable life or to simply survive. We all should plan for and pick our profession carefully and work hard to land our dream jobs. There are no other ways around it, and we have to face it head on.

Nothing is free, not in this country, not in this world. Bad news. It all costs money to have a clean and cozy home to return to at night in a safe neighborhood, to afford quality food with balanced nutrients, to have a great night out at a sports bars with friends, to travel to enjoy Caribbean or Hawaiian beaches, to bathe in the sunshine in southern Europe, to watch wild animals roaming in the African safari, or to immerse ourselves in exotic cultures in Asia.

Needless to say, this list can go on and on: Driving a dream car, having the latest gadgets without too much agonizing over the price, affording hobbies for us and our family, purchasing nice birthday and holiday gifts for family, friends, and coworkers.

Fortunately, we live in a country where a stable social and political system exists. Let us be clear about and be proud of it: Although far from perfect, the United States of America as a country runs pretty well, far better than a lot of other countries around the globe that are plagued by war, poverty, poor public health, corruption, and a lack of social, economic, and spiritual liberty.

As a citizen, an immigrant, or a foreign worker with a legitimate visa in the U.S., all of the above about leading a comfortable life can be available and within reach to us, if we have a decent job. With a nicely paying job, we will be able to afford all the above typical costs and expenses associated with living in America, and bring the American dream to reality.

Life can be wonderful with a wonderful job.

On the flip side, life can be miserable if we do not have a good paying, secure job.

None of the above about a cozy home, hanging out with friends, traveling to beautiful places, having nice cars or latest models of cell phones will happen to us. None. We will be watching others living a great life, only with ourselves stuck in misery.

So, we've got to have a job, a good one. Now, here are the questions for ourselves:

Out of the hundreds of different professions, which one do we choose?

Which job will bring in sufficient income to meet our financial needs?

Which job will be a stable one and will not get us worried about losing it in a couple of years?

These are not easy questions to answer. In fact, these are tough, million-dollar questions. Aiming for the right job is paramount; mistakes will be costly.

To drive this point home, let us work out a simple example to illustrate how expensive the above questions are.

According to the latest employment data collected by the U.S. Department of Labor, an average worker, among all the 156 million people working a job in the U.S. across all the 820 occupations, earns a salary of $37,040 per year.

Let us use this typical annual salary to calculate a rough, maybe very rough, estimate of the total dollar amount we would make before retirement as an average worker in the U.S.

To form the estimate, let us assume that we start working at age 22. Although many of us start working jobs before age 22, there is no need to be overly precise for our purposes here. Rough, ballpark numbers will deliver the point just fine. Thus, let us just be content about using 22 as the starting age in our calculation.

Let us also assume that we work till retirement at 62 years old. This assumption is reasonable, as the earliest time we can receive Social Security benefits is at 62. Social Security is the commonly used term for the federal Old-Age, Survivors, and Disability Insurance (OASDI) program in the U.S., including retirement benefits.

Between age 22 and age 62, it is 40 years of working jobs, making $37,040 per year for an average worker. Multiply $37,040 per year by 40 years give us a total sum of lifetime earnings of $1,481,600.

According to the above calculation, an average person, regardless of age, gender, education, work location, and occupation, will make a cumulative lifetime salary of $1,481,600 before retirement.

Let us emphasize here that the $1,481,600 figure is definitely an underestimate of an average person's lifetime earnings, for a couple of reasons.

First, many of us start working jobs way before age 22, while some of us will continue working jobs way after the retirement age of 62.

Second, many of the smart readers might have noticed that in the above calculation, we factored in no inflation. This is unrealistic, as there always is inflation.

Over a course of 40 years, inflation can drastically change the annual income. Therefore, ignoring inflation produces vastly lower estimate of how much we will make in the next 40 years. If we take inflation into account, our lifetime earnings will surely be more than $1,481,600.

Just for the fun of it, let us see if we factor in inflation, what would the lifetime earnings be.

The long term annual inflation rate in the U.S. over the past 100 years is 3.22%. Let us assume this is going to the inflation rate every year for the next 40 years. With this pace of inflation, our total earnings over the next 40 years balloons up to $2,936,357. That is nearly 3 million dollars.

Thus, the above questions about choosing a profession do indeed turn out to be million-dollar questions. By million dollars, we are not exaggerating at all. In fact, they are more likely 3-million-dollar questions, if we factor into our calculation inflations in the years to come.

Very expensive questions to answer, very expensive decisions to make, and very serious reasons to motivate us to choose our profession wisely. If we are successful in doing so, we will enjoy financial success and attain peace of mind, knowing that we have the ability to take care of family and friends whom we love and care about.

If, instead, we end up with making an unwise decision, it could not only lead to lifelong financial struggles but also take a toll on our emotional and mental health.

It could be depressing and heartbreaking when we realize that our job will never be stable. We will be forced to constantly move on and will never be paid enough to meet our financial needs. Anticipating that our job is going to disappear in near future will for sure cast a long and unwavering shadow in our mind.

Why This Book

"Knowledge is power," says the English philosopher Francis Bacon. The more reliable the knowledge, the more powerful it becomes.

When it comes to the serious matter of choosing a profession, decisions should not be attempted lightly. We should refrain from rushing into any quick decisions, as our decisions will make or break our American dreams.

Instead, it pays off handsomely if we equip ourselves with comprehensive knowledge of and key insights into what is available to us in the labor markets. We will certainly be better off this way in striving to make a best career choice.

This book, America's Best Jobs, provides us with such crucial knowledge and insights, to help us answer the million-dollar questions raised above which are also repeated here:

Out of the hundreds of different professions, which one do we choose?

Which jobs will bring in sufficient income to meet our financial needs?

Which jobs are stable ones and will not get us worried about losing it in a couple of years?

With the right answers to these questions, we will be standing on a solid ground in making informed and wise career choices.

A decision made this way is much more likely to be able to stand the test of time, without becoming one decision that we will regret later in our life.

The knowledge and insights offered in this book are derived and distilled from the employment information covering 156 million jobs across 820 occupations in the U.S. These 820 occupations are grouped into 22 major occupation groups.

Later in this book, we will go through a lot of details about these major occupation groups as well as the detailed occupations within these major groups.

Mentioned already earlier in this book, this employment information is sourced from the U.S. Department of Labor, doubtlessly the most comprehensive and most authoritative source of employment information. No other source, in public or private domains, could come anywhere close.

Furthermore, the wage information from this source is very up to date, just released in May 2017. And the job growth outlook forecasted for the 10-year period of 2016 to 2026 was released only in October 2017. These latest pieces of information reflect the very current state of affairs, as far as jobs are concerned.

Garbage in, Garbage out. No, we do not want to base our career decisions on obsolete information. In this book, there is no garbage information but only comprehensive, accurate, and up to date information that we can confidently base our decisions upon.

Sourcing the most comprehensive and most authoritative employment data is only the starting point. The sourced data needs to be sliced, diced, and digested to become useful.

Only when the data is processed and understood can insights come out of it. On top of all of these, the insights need to be organized and presented in an easy to understand fashion. And only then, Voilà! This book was finally born!

With this book, you do not need to worry about the quality, freshness, and comprehensiveness of the employment information you need for making wise career decisions. You do what needs your attention most, *making decisions*. The invaluable information provided in this book helps you make sound ones.

All the priceless information and insights are now at your disposal in this book, at the mere cost of a couple cups of coffee or a quick bite for lunch in town, to aid your decision that is worth millions of dollars and a quality life that you will be able to afford as a result of reading through this book.

What Aspects of Jobs Are Covered

The next chapter in this book introduces to us the kinds of occupations available to us in the labor market here in the U.S. Our choice of occupation is such a serious matter that we do not want to make blind decision. Only with the illumination of the knowledge of what is available out there can we make a decision that is going to best suit our individual needs.

In the same chapter, we reveal stunning differences in salaries and substantial differences in job growth outlook, across major groups of occupations. Salary and growth look are among key considerations that all of us have in mind when choosing occupations.

Chapter 3 of the book pin points the top three most important underlying factors that drive eye-opening occupational differences. These 3 factors are: Education, education and education.

Our education attainment level determines to a large extent the size of the salary we are able to make at a job. This chapter shows us the real dollar numbers that workers make, for different levels of education attainment, to enable a clear comparison and motivate us to pursue as much education as possible.

Time, effort, tuition, and other expenses invested in education will pay off easily and quickly. Before we eagerly jump into the labor market, it would be only profitable to plan our career and life well first, with education a critical part of the plan.

In addition to salary differences, Chapter 3 also presents the disparities in unemployment rate and growth outlook by education level.

Other than education, another key factor driving wage disparities is location, the topic in Chapter 4. The availability of jobs and the salaries that jobs pay both vary greatly between states and cities due to their population, geographical location which is key to commerce, level of local economic development, and concentration of certain industries.

Chapter 4 lays in front of our eyes the numbers of available jobs and their wages, not only between states but also between major metropolitan areas in the country. For those of us who are willing to relocate away from hometown, read this chapter carefully and direct our energy to search for jobs in the states and cities that offer more attractive jobs than in our hometown.

Starting from Chapter 5, we dive into detailed occupation ranking. In this chapter, we find out about the top 100 best paying jobs: What are they? And how much do they pay?

The jobs are ranked by the typical salary paid to an average worker in an occupation. In addition, for each ranked occupation, we also present salaries that are likely paid to top performers, showing the earnings potential if we excel at our jobs.

In Chapter 6, we focus on a particular aspect of job security: Job growth outlook between 2016 and 2026. We all want a job whose demand for workers gets stronger over time. This chapter identifies the top 100 fastest growing jobs in the U.S.

The importance of a robust growth of demand for a job is self-evident. Just imagine a situation where we know our jobs are going downhill and are going to disappear in several years. What kind of stress that would put in our mind for those years, and then we lose our jobs after enduring those years! A horrific picture that we do not want to be in any part of it.

Some jobs are indeed fast disappearing, and we need to know what they are to steer clear of entering those dying occupations without knowing their gloomy future. In Chapter 7, we find out what these sunset jobs are. A misstep here can be very costly. This chapter helps us play defense and navigate through the minefield of vanishing jobs.

Salary, growth outlook, job location, and education requirements are most important aspects of jobs that we all should take into account in choosing a profession. It is the author's sincere hope that the reader finds information provided in Chapters 2 to 7 in the book valuable in making sound career choices.

What Else Other Than Salary and Outlook

It needs to be stressed that although salary, growth outlook, job location, education requirements information provided in this book is priceless in helping make the right career choices, the readers are advised strongly not to base their decisions solely on these factors.

It would be prudent for us to also consider other critical aspects of going into a profession. For instance, are we truly interested in taking up a particular profession? A profession might be secure and pay well, but if it is something that we always hate to do, do not go there.

Furthermore, do not attempt an occupation that is way north of our caliber. For example, rocket scientists sound cool and are paid well. However, if we have trouble getting A's in high school math classes, it is better not to try out the profession of rocket scientists. It will prove a colossal mistake.

We all have our own strengths and weaknesses; just be sure to know ourselves and form strategies to efficiently leverage our strengths but play defense on weaknesses instead of exposing them.

In addition, consider the investment of money, time, and effort that we have to make before we can land a particular job. Are we willing and able to make these investments?

As an example, it is well known that medical doctors make a ton of money and do not seem to have trouble finding a job anywhere.

However, becoming a doctor requires going through

tough and very expensive medical school years. After the medical school, one has to become a resident doctor first, and then sometimes a fellow physician after residency, before finally reaching the rank of staff physicians.

The years are long, and workload is demanding, often requiring 24/7 on call. Although becoming a physician can lead to a very rewarding career, this level of investment of money and years of time, together with the sacrifice of personal life, might not be the right choice for some of us.

Therefore, in addition to wage, job growth outlook, job location, and education requirements information found in this book, we should consider at least these additional factors: Whether we are genuinely interested in an occupation, whether we possess or can acquire physical and intellectual aptitude to excel in a job, and whether we are willing and able to make investments required to get ready for the job.

In Chapter 8, we will learn a systematic method to stitch together all the considerations mentioned above, including salary, job growth outlook, job location, level of interest in the job, aptitude required to do the job well, and the level of investment (including investment in education) we need to make before landing a job.

This systematic method is smart in combining all these considerations into a simple score, to enable us to evaluate and compare candidate jobs on an apple-to-apple basis.

We can easily adjust the parameters of the method to cater to our individual preferences and needs, to calculate a job score that is personalized according to our individual situations.

In contrast, other job rankings that can be found elsewhere are not personalized, either not reflecting the considerations we care, or weighting them in a way we do not agree, or both.

With the personalized job scores at our disposal for all candidate jobs we are considering, we maximize our chance of making a wise career decision that best suits our own situation.

Chapter 9, a short and the final chapter of the book, points the reader to additional information on occupations, including where to obtain a full list of all 820 occupations, each with the typical wage, job growth outlook, and more.

***

For those of us who are about to enter the workforce, it is now high time to read through this book to get ourselves started in learning about hundreds of occupation choices available in the labor market across the country, before we dive into the job market blindly.

It is also high time to learn how to compare occupations in a consistent, systematic, and personalized way, by applying the personalized job score method taught in this book.

For those of us who are already employed, it is also important to read through this book to discover how our current job stacks up against other options.

We should ask ourselves this question: Are there other jobs within our reach that would pay much more, have a much brighter future, or both? This book helps us answer this question. If the answer is yes, we might want to seriously consider making career changes.

The little time and effort we spend now studying this book will result in much better career choices and will pay off themselves thousands of times over.

2 JOBS ARE NOT CREATED EQUAL

When I was 5 years old, my mother always told me that happiness was the key to life. When I went to school, they asked me what I wanted to be when I grew up. I wrote down 'happy'. They told me I didn't understand the assignment, and I told them they didn't understand life.

— *John Lennon*

This question is timeless and gets asked a lot everyday: What do you want to be when you grow up? No doubt that many of us have been asked this very question growing up, and children around the globe are still being asked this very same question in hundreds of languages.

We have heard answers ranging from ordinary ones: "I want to be a fireman (policeman, soldier, nurse, singer, teacher, etc.)!" to funny ones: "I want to be like Mommy!",

"I want to be a tree!" (a tree?), "I want to be eight!" (when asked when the child was seven), to fantasies: "I want to be Spiderman (Batman, Power Ranger, Cinderella, Dora, a Princess)!"

It is apparent that children picked characters they knew of at the time when they were asked this question. Now kids' stuff aside, when we attempt to make a career path decision, it is super important for us to know what occupations are out there.

How could we ever make sound decisions if we did not even know about available options?

In this chapter, let us find out together what occupations are available here in the U.S. labor market, and then let us look at eye-opening differences between the occupations, focusing on the wages these occupations pay to the workers, as well as job growth outlook.

The primary goal of this chapter is to reveal the occupational landscape in the United States. To this end, although we will talk about some individual occupations in this chapter, we focus analyses here more on the so-called major occupation groups, each of which contains typically dozens of similar individual occupations.

In this chapter, we first introduce briefly the origin of the major occupation groups and the sizes of these major groups, in terms of the number of workers employed in the groups.

We then provide a full list of the major occupation groups, ranked by the typical salary paid within each group, in the remainder of the chapter.

Twenty-Two Major Occupation Groups

There are literally hundreds of professions. According to the classification system used by the U.S. Department of Labor as of 2017, there are 820 occupations, classified into 22 major occupation groups. The occupations within a group are similar with respect to the tasks and duties performed and the skills possessed by the incumbents.

The U.S. Department of Labor operates a comprehensive database covering all the 156 million job positions in the U.S. The database is updated on a periodic basis. No question that this is the most authoritative and credible source for labor related information in the U.S.

Just a small note to the reader. Although the information cited in this chapter was released in 2017 and is the latest available in 2017, the information itself is as of May 2016.

The time discrepancy is easy to understand: It takes time for the Department of Labor to collect information as of May 2016, process it, analyze it, and then release it in 2017.

To be entirely accurate, the occupation classification actually consists of 23 major groups. However, only 22 were included in the data released by the U.S. Department of

Labor. A 23rd major occupation group of Military Specific Occupations was not covered in the data release. Due to this data limitation, this book covers only 22 major groups excluding the Military Specific Occupations group.

The major occupation group that employs the largest number of workers is the group of Office and Administrative Support Occupations, counting 23.1 million workers or 15% of the total 156 million workforce in the U.S.

Typical occupations within the group are general office clerks, customer service representatives, secretaries and administrative assistants (except legal, medical, and executive), stock clerks and order fillers, bookkeeping/accounting/auditing clerks, and first-line supervisors of office and administrative support workers.

The number of workers employed in the group of Sales and Related Occupations ranks the second, counting 15.7 million or roughly 10% of the total 156 million.

Typical occupations within the group include retail salespersons, cashiers, wholesale and manufacturing sales representatives (except technical and scientific products), and first-line supervisors of retail sales workers.

Ranked in the 3rd place, in terms of the workers employed, is the major group of Food Preparation and Service Related Occupations.

There are 13.2 million workers taking up these

occupations, accounting for 8% of the total 156 million workforce in the U.S.

Typical occupations within the group include combined food preparation and serving workers, waiters and waitresses, restaurant or fast food cooks, first-line supervisors of food preparation and serving workers, food preparation workers, and bartenders.

These three major occupation groups account for a total of 33% of the workers in the U.S. See Figure 1 for a comparison between the major groups ranked #1 to #11, in terms of the percentage of the total workforce. These 11 groups make up 77% of the total number of jobs.

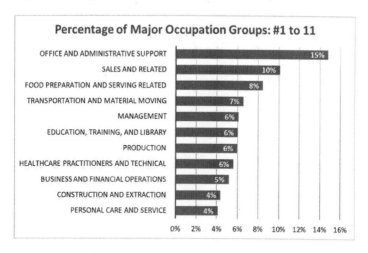

Figure 1. Percentage of Major Occupation Groups: #1 to 11

Another comparison chart between the remaining major groups ranked #12 to #22 is shown in Figure 2. Notice that the two charts have difference horizontal scales.

In Figure 2, the total percentage of the major groups there account for only 23% of the total workforces, much smaller than that of 77% in Figure 1.

The smallest major occupation group is the group of Farming, Fishing and Forestry occupations, counting slightly more than a million workers.

Typical occupations in this group include farmworkers and laborers, agricultural products graders and sorters, agricultural equipment operators, and logging equipment operators.

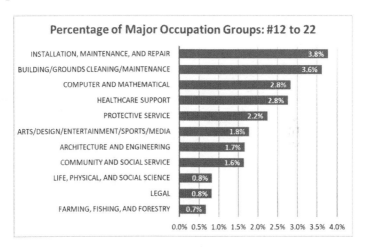

Figure 2. Percentage of Major Occupation Groups: #12 to 22

Now we have learned about the 22 major occupation groups in the U.S. Of course, the tasks and duties are very different between these occupation groups, as well as their relative workforce sizes.

Next, before we present the full list of the 22 major occupation groups, we will introduce a statistical term, the median salary.

What Is the Median Salary

In everyday language, when we say the *median salary* of an occupation, the occupation of secretaries for instance, we mean the *typical* salary paid to secretaries. Or equivalently, by the *median salary*, we mean the *salary paid to an average worker* (secretary in this example).

Therefore, for all purposes in this book, median salary = typical salary = salary paid to an average worker.

If you do not feel like going through the remaining of this brief section below for a more precise definition of the median salary, you can skip it but just remember whenever you see "the median salary" in this book, you can substitute it with either "the typical salary" or "the salary paid to an average worker".

That will do the trick and would not cause any loss in understanding the messages in the book. Take the "Get Out of Jail Free" card now, and skip to the next section if you like.

If you decided to stick around and learn more about the definition of the median salary, here is a more precise definition. The median is the midpoint (a number, or salary in our case here, in the middle) of a bunch of numbers such that among the remaining numbers, half are smaller than the midpoint, while the other half numbers are greater than this midpoint.

The concept of the median can be better grasped with the assistance of an example. Suppose we have 5 workers: Alice, Bob, Charlie, Dylan, and Ethan, making $10, $20, $30, $40, and $900 per hour, respectively.

Now that we have these 5 numbers, applying the median definition above, we know that the wage of $30 that Charlie makes is the median among the 5 numbers. This is because 2 numbers ($10 and $20) are less than $30, while 2 other numbers ($40, $900) are greater than it.

Because Charlie is in the middle of the five people in this example, it is easy to see why loosely we think the median salary is the typical salary, as all other salaries are split into two groups around this number: One group below it and the other above it.

It also makes sense to think that the median salary is the salary paid to an average worker, again because the earner of the median salary, Charlie, lies right in the middle of the 5 workers here in this example who are ranked by salary they make. Supposedly, Charlies is more valuable a worker than Alice and Bob, but less so than Dylan and Ethan, and thus is an average worker.

However, one subtlety is that the median salary is *not* the average salary, and they can be very different. Using this example again, the average salary between the 5 workers here is actually $200, calculated by summing the 5 numbers of $10, $20, 30, $40, and $900 first, and then divide the sum ($1,000) by 5 workers.

Thus, the *average* salary is $200, much more than the median salary of $30. The average salary is dragged off by the top earner in this example, Ethan, who makes $900 per hour, a much higher salary than those of the other four people.

We prefer to use the median salary instead of the average salary to compare different occupations, as we would like to avoid the undue bias introduced by a few top earners.

For example, a salary of $1 million earned by a CEO will drag off the average salary considerably, but it has nothing to anybody other than the CEO herself.

On the contrary, the median salary is much more indicative of the salaries that ordinary workers expect to take home.

The astute reader might already have a question forming in the head: What if, in the above example, there are only four workers? What would be the median?

Good question.

Suppose now we have only four workers: Alice, Bob,

Charlie and Dylan (but no more Ethan), making $10, $20, $30, and $40 per hour, respectively.

In this case, no wage out of the above four wages can separate the four wages into two equal groups. So, we take the middle two: $20 and $30, calculate the average ($25) of the two, and then declare $25 to be the median.

Hence this artificial wage of $25 becomes the midpoint that separates $10, $20, $30 and $40 into two equal halves, one half less than $25 and the other half greater than $25.

OK, this is it. This is all we need to know about what the median salary is.

Occupation Groups Ranked by Salary

Below presents the full list of the 22 major occupation groups in America, ranked by the median wages in these major groups in a descending order. For each major group, we report also the two occupations paying the highest and lowest wages within the group, respectively.

In addition, we provide the 10-year growth outlook for each major occupation group, projected for the period of 2016 to 2026.

The average growth across all occupations during the 10 years is forecasted to be 7.4%. Keep this number in mind, and use it to measure whether or not an occupation group will outpace this average growth.

Going through all the major occupation groups, the reader gets to develop a level of familiarity with the occupation landscape here in America, and form a general idea of what the occupations are, how much they typically pay, and what growth outlook the future holds for them.

1. Management Occupations

(Median wage: $100,790; 10-year growth: 9.2%)

Counting 6% of the total 156 million workforce in the U.S., workers in the management occupations group are paid a median annual wage (meaning the wage paid to an average person) of $100,790 in May 2016, which was the highest median wage among all the major occupation groups.

This makes sense. Once assuming managerial responsibilities, we will be making greater contributions to the employers, and as a consequence, we will be rewarded more.

This is a large occupation group, consisting of 34 detailed occupations. Top occupations within the group that employ a large number of workers include, for example, general and operations managers, financial managers, sales managers, computer and information systems managers, medical and health services managers, administrative services managers, construction managers, education administrators, chief executives, marketing managers, food service managers, real estate and community association managers, architectural and engineering managers, industrial production managers, human resources managers, social and community service managers, transportation, storage, and distribution managers, purchasing managers, public relations and fundraising managers, among many others.

Among all occupations within the management occupations major group, an average **chief executive** earns $181,210 annually, the highest within the group. An average **legislator** takes home $23,470 annually, the lowest within this major group.

Over the 2016 to 2026 period, the occupations within this group together are projected to grow 9.2%, faster than the average growth of 7.4% across all occupations.

2. **Computer and Mathematical Occupations**

(Median wage: $82,830; 10-year growth: 13.5%)

Counting only 3% of the total 156 million workforce in the U.S., workers in the group of computer and mathematical occupations are paid a median annual wage of $82,830, the second highest median wage of all the major occupation groups.

This occupation group consists of 19 detailed occupations. Computer occupations within the group include software developers, computer user support specialists, computer systems analysts, network and computer systems administrators, computer network architects, web developers, database administrators, information security analysts, and computer and information research scientists.

Mathematical occupations within the group include operations research analysts, statisticians, actuaries, and mathematicians.

Among all occupations within this major group, an average **computer and information research scientist** earns $111,840 annually, the highest within the group. An average **computer user support specialist** takes home $49,390 annually, the lowest within this major group. Even this lowest paying occupation earns significantly more than the all-occupation median salary of $37,040.

Over the 2016 to 2026 period, the occupations within this group together are projected to grow 13.5%, nearly twice as fast as the average growth of 7.4% across all occupations.

High paying, and fast growing. Sounds like a perfect combination that we are looking for!

3. **Legal Occupations**

(Median wage: $79,650; 10-year growth: 9.8%)

Counting only 1% of the total 156 million workforce in the U.S., workers in the group of legal occupations are paid a median annual wage of $79,650, the third highest median wage of all the major occupation groups.

This occupation group employs only slightly more than 1 million workers. Across all 22 groups, only the farming, fishing, and forestry occupations group employs fewer workers.

This group consists of only 9 detailed occupations, including lawyers, paralegals and legal assistants, title examiners/ abstractors/ searchers, other legal support workers, judges/ magistrate judges/ magistrates, court reporters, administrative law judges/ adjudicators/ hearing officers, judicial law clerks, and arbitrators/ mediators/ conciliators.

Judges, magistrate judges, and magistrates earn a typical salary of $125,880 annually, the highest within this major group. Average **title examiners, abstractors, and searchers** take home $45,800 annually, the lowest within this major group. Even this lowest paying occupation earns significantly more than the all-occupation median salary of $37,040.

It is a little surprising that lawyers make a typical salary of $118,160, nowhere near the top and contrary to the general perception. A salary of $118,160 is not bad in any way, but typical lawyers do not seem to fly in the same echelon as anesthesiologists who typically take home $247,000, as far as salary is concerned.

The reason might be that anesthesiologists are a much more select group than lawyers. In the U.S., while there are only 33,000 anesthesiologists, there are 26 times as many lawyers and judges (858,200). A typical lawyer earns a salary far below a typical anesthesiologist, but the really good lawyers probably make a lot more, much closer to the salary of anesthesiologists.

Over the 2016 to 2026 period, the occupations within this group together are projected to grow 9.8%, faster than the average growth of 7.4% across all occupations.

4. **Architecture and Engineering Occupations**

(Median wage: $77,900; 10-year growth: 7.4%)

Counting only 2% of the total 156 million workforce in the U.S., workers in the group of architecture and engineering occupations are paid a median annual wage of $77,900.

Consisting of 35 detailed occupations, this large major occupation group includes jobs across all walks of engineering. Top occupations within the group that employ a large number of workers are civil engineers and technicians, mechanical engineers and technicians, industrial engineers and technicians, electrical engineers, electronics engineers (except computer), architects (except landscape and naval), architectural and civil drafters, engineering technicians, computer hardware engineers, aerospace engineers, mechanical drafters, surveying and mapping technicians, and environmental engineers.

Average **petroleum engineers** earn a salary of $128,230 annually, the highest within this major group. Average **surveying and mapping technicians** take home $42,450 annually, the lowest within this major group.

Over the 2016 to 2026 period, the occupations within this group together are projected to grow 7.4%, on a par with the average growth of 7.4% across all occupations.

5. **Business and Financial Operations Occupations**

(Median wage: $66,530; 10-year growth: 9.3%)

Counting 5% of the total 156 million workforce in the U.S., workers in the group of business and financial operations occupations are paid a median wage of $66,530.

Consisting of 32 detailed occupations, this is also a large major occupation group. Top occupations within the group that employ a large number of workers are accountants and auditors, business operations specialists, management analysts, market research analysts and marketing specialists, human resources specialists, loan officers, purchasing agents, financial analysts, claims adjusters, examiners, and investigators, compliance officers, training and development specialists, cost estimators, and personal financial advisors.

Average **personal financial advisors** earn a salary of $90,530 annually, the highest within this major group. Average **farm labor contractors** take home $35,160 annually, the lowest within this major group which is slightly below the all-occupation median salary of $37,040.

Over the 2016 to 2026 period, the occupations within this group together are projected to grow 9.3%, faster than the average growth of 7.4% across all occupations.

6. **Healthcare Practitioners and Technical Occupations**

(Median wage: $63,420; 10-year growth: 15.2%)

Counting 6% of the total 156 million workforce in the U.S., workers in the group of healthcare practitioners and technical occupations are paid a median wage of $63,420.

A very large major occupation group consisting of 61 detailed occupations, the group includes many healthcare jobs. Ranked by the number of workers in the occupation from high to low, top occupations within the group are registered nurses, licensed practical and licensed vocational nurses, pharmacists and pharmacy technicians, physicians and surgeons, emergency medical technicians and paramedics, physical therapists, dentists and dental hygienists, radiologic technologists, medical records and health information technicians, medical and clinical laboratory technologists, medical and clinical laboratory technicians, nurse practitioners, speech-language pathologists, respiratory therapists, family and general practitioners, health technologists and technicians, occupational therapists, surgical technologists, physician assistants, veterinary technologists and technicians, and occupational health and safety specialists.

Average **anesthesiologists** earn a salary of $247,339 annually, the highest within this major group. As discussed earlier, anesthesiologists are *the* top earners across all occupations.

Average **dietetic technicians** take home $26,350 annually, the lowest within this major group which is much lower than the all-occupation median salary of $37,040.

With this major occupation group, the gap between the highest and the lowest median salaries is staggering!

Over the 2016 to 2026 period, the occupations within this group together are projected to grow 15.2%, more than twice as fast as the average growth of 7.4% across all occupations.

This projected growth of 15.2% is the third highest, only after those of the healthcare support occupations (23.2% growth) and personal care and service occupations (18.2% growth), over the same 10-year period.

7. Life, Physical, and Social Science Occupations

(Median wage: $63,340; 10-year growth: 9.5%)

Counting a tiny 1% of the total 156 million workforce in the U.S., workers in the group of life, physical, and social science occupations are paid a median wage of $63,340.

Consisting of 43 detailed occupations, this major group includes medical scientists, psychologists, chemists and chemical technicians, environmental scientists and specialists, biological scientists and technicians, life, physical, and social science technicians, social scientists and related workers, urban and regional planners, environmental science and protection technicians, geoscientists, forest and conservation technicians, social science research assistants, biochemists and biophysicists, microbiologists, conservation scientists, agricultural and food science technicians, economists, zoologists and wildlife biologists, physicists, geological and petroleum technicians, and forensic science technicians.

Average **physicists** earn a salary of $115,870 annually, the highest within this major group. Average **forest and conservation technicians** take home $35,560 annually, the lowest within this major group and slightly below the all-occupation median salary.

Over the 2016 to 2026 period, the occupations within this group together are projected to grow 9.5%, faster than the average growth of 7.4% across all occupations.

8. **Education, Training, and Library Occupations**

    (Median wage: $48,000; 10-year growth: 9.3%)

    Counting 6% of the total 156 million workforce in the U.S., workers in the group of education, training, and library occupations are paid a median wage of $48,000.

    Consisting of 64 detailed occupations, this large major group includes elementary and secondary school teachers, teacher assistants, substitute teachers, kindergarten and preschool teachers, self-enrichment education teachers, postsecondary teachers, special education teachers, postsecondary health specialties teachers, instructional coordinators, graduate teaching assistants, librarians, vocational education teachers, postsecondary art, drama, and music teachers, and library technicians.

    Average **postsecondary law teachers** earn a salary of $111,210 annually, the highest within this major group.

Average **teacher assistants** take home $25,410 annually, the lowest within this major group.

Over the 2016 to 2026 period, the occupations within this group together are projected to grow 9.3%, faster than the average growth of 7.4% across all occupations.

9. **Arts, Design, Entertainment, Sports, and Media Occupations**

(Median wage: $47,190; 10-year growth: 6.3%)

Counting only 2% of the total 156 million workforce in the U.S., workers in the group of arts, design, entertainment, sports, and media occupations are paid a median wage of $47,190.

Consisting of 41 detailed occupations, this large major group includes coaches and scouts, public relations specialists, graphic designers, merchandise displayers and window trimmers, producers and directors, editors, audio and video equipment technicians, interior designers, interpreters and translators, technical writers, photographers, actors, writers and authors, floral designers, musicians and singers, reporters and correspondents, art directors, commercial and industrial designers, broadcast technicians, film and video editors, multimedia artists and animators, radio and television announcers, media and communication workers, television and motion picture camera operators, fashion designers, umpires, referees, and other sports officials, and music directors and composers.

Average **art directors** earn a salary of $89,820 annually, the highest within this major group. Average **umpires, referees, and other sports officials** take home $25,660 annually, the lowest within this major group and much lower than the all-occupation median salary of $37,040.

Over the 2016 to 2026 period, the occupations within this group together are projected to grow 6.3%, modestly slower than the average growth of 7.4% across all occupations.

10. Construction and Extraction Occupations

(Median wage: $43,610; 10-year growth: 11.1%)

Counting 4% of the total 156 million workforce in the U.S., workers in the group of construction and extraction occupations are paid a median wage of $43,610.

Consisting of 60 detailed occupations, this large major group includes construction laborers, carpenters, electricians, first-line supervisors of construction trades and extraction workers, plumbers, pipefitters, and steamfitters, operating engineers and other construction equipment operators, painters, cement masons and concrete finishers, highway maintenance workers, sheet metal workers, roofers, construction and building inspectors, drywall and ceiling tile installers, electricians helpers, structural iron and steel workers, and brick masons and block masons, pipe layers helpers.

Average **elevator installers and repairers** earn a salary of $78,890 annually, the highest within this major group. Average **helpers to painters, paperhangers, plasterers, and stucco masons** take home $27,310 annually, the lowest within this major group.

Over the 2016 to 2026 period, the occupations within this group together are projected to grow 11.1%, much faster than the average growth of 7.4% across all occupations.

11. Installation, Maintenance, and Repair Occupations

(Median wage: $43,440; 10-year growth: 6.7%)

Counting 4% of the total 156 million workforce in the U.S., workers in the group of installation, maintenance, and repair occupations are paid a median salary of $43,440.

Consisting of 52 detailed occupations, this large major group includes maintenance and repair workers, automotive service technicians and mechanics, first-line supervisors of mechanics, installers, and repairers, industrial machinery mechanics, heating, air conditioning, and refrigeration mechanics and installers, bus and truck mechanics and diesel engine specialists, telecommunications equipment installers and repairers, automotive body and related repairers, aircraft mechanics and service technicians, mobile heavy equipment mechanics, electrical power-line installers and repairers, tire repairers and changers, computer, automated teller, and office machine repairers, telecommunications line installers and repairers, machinery maintenance workers, security and fire alarm systems installers, electrical and electronics repairers, and control and valve installers and repairers.

Average **electrical and electronics repairers** make a salary of $75,670 annually, the highest within this major group. Average **tire repairers and changers** take home $25,040 annually, the lowest within this major group.

Over the 2016 to 2026 period, the occupations within this group together are projected to grow 6.7%, slower than the average growth of 7.4% across all occupations.

12. Community and Social Service Occupations

(Median wage: $42,990; 10-year growth: 13.5%)

Counting only 2% of the total 156 million workforce in the U.S., workers in the group of community and social service occupations are paid a median salary of $42,990.

This major group consists of only 18 detailed

occupations, including social and human service assistants, school social workers (for children, families, and schools), educational counselors, healthcare social workers, mental health counselors, substance abuse social workers, rehabilitation counselors, community and social service specialists, substance abuse and behavioral disorder counselors, probation officers and correctional treatment specialists, health educators, community health workers, clergy, marriage and family therapists, religious activities and education directors, and religious workers.

An average **social worker** earns $60,230 annually, the highest within this major group. Average **miscellaneous religious workers** take home $28,820 annually, the lowest within this major group.

Over the 2016 to 2026 period, the occupations within this group together are projected to grow 13.5%, much more briskly than the average growth of 7.4% across all occupations.

13. Protective Service Occupations

(Median wage: $38,660; 10-year growth: 4.5%)

Counting only 2% of the total 156 million workforce in the U.S., workers in the group of protective service occupations are paid a median wage of $38,660.

This major group consists of only 18 detailed

occupations, including security guards, police and sheriff's patrol officers, correctional officers and jailers, firefighters, lifeguards, ski patrol, other recreational protective service workers, detectives and criminal investigators, first-line supervisors of police and detectives, crossing guards, first-line supervisors of fire-fighting and prevention workers, first-line supervisors of correctional officers, transportation security screeners, private detectives and investigators, bailiffs, animal control workers, fire inspectors and investigators, gaming surveillance officers and gaming investigators, parking enforcement workers, fish and game wardens, transit and railroad police, forest fire inspectors and prevention specialists.

An average **first-line supervisor of police and detectives** earns $84,840 annually, the highest within this major group. Average lifeguards, **ski patrol, and other recreational protective service workers** take home $20,290 annually, the lowest within this major group.

Over the 2016 to 2026 period, the occupations within this group together are projected to grow 4.5%, much slower than the average growth of 7.4% across all occupations.

All Occupations: The median wage for all occupations is $37,040. An average person in all major occupation groups already presented above makes more than this figure, while an average person in all major occupation groups listed below makes less.

In terms of growth outlook, the average growth outlook across all occupations is 7.4%, projected for 10-year period of 2016 to 2026.

14. Office and Administrative Support Occupations

(Median wage: $34,050; 10-year growth: 0.6%)

Counting 15% of the total 156 million workforce in the U.S., workers in the group of office and administrative support occupations are paid a median wage of $34,050.

This is the largest major occupation group in term of the sheer number of workers employed, 22 million, spreading across 56 detailed occupations.

These occupations include general office clerks, customer service representatives, secretaries and administrative assistants, stock clerks and order fillers, bookkeeping, accounting, and auditing clerks, first-line supervisors of office and administrative support workers, receptionists and information clerks, shipping, receiving, and traffic clerks, medical secretaries, tellers, billing and posting clerks, postal service mail carriers, production, planning, and expediting clerks, bill and account collectors, insurance claims and policy processing clerks, hotel, motel, and resort desk clerks, loan interviewers and clerks, dispatchers (except police, fire, and ambulance), data entry keyers, interviewers, order clerks, payroll and timekeeping clerks, and reservation and transportation ticket agents and travel clerks.

An average **postal service mail carrier** earns $58,110 annually for an average person, the highest within this major group. Average **hotel, motel, and resort desk clerks** take home $22,070 annually, the lowest within this major group.

Over the 2016 to 2026 period, the occupations within this group together are projected to grow only 0.6%, much more sluggish than the average growth of 7.4% across all occupations. In other words, it is not much job growth at all, but staying rather flat essentially between 2016 and 2026.

15. Production Occupations

(Median wage: $33,130; 10-year growth: -4.1%)

Counting 6% of the total 156 million workforce in the U.S., workers in the group of production occupations are paid a median wage of $33,130.

This is the largest major occupation group in term of the sheer number of detailed occupations within this group, 108 of them.

The occupations in this group include for example team

assemblers, first-line supervisors of production and operating workers, inspectors, testers, sorters, samplers, and weighers, machinists, packaging and filling machine operators, welders, cutters, solderers, and brazers, assemblers and fabricators, electrical and electronic equipment assemblers, laundry and dry-cleaning workers, cutting, punching, and press machine operators, bakers, printing press operators, meat, poultry, and fish cutters and trimmers, food batchmakers, computer-controlled machine tool operators, molding, coremaking, and casting machine operators, sewing machine operators, butchers and meat cutters, mixing and blending machine operators, water and wastewater treatment plant and system operators, and cabinetmakers and bench carpenters.

An average **nuclear power reactor operator** earns $91,170 annually, the highest within this major group. Average **pressers for textile, garment, and related materials** take home $21,300 annually, the lowest within this major group.

Over the 2016 to 2026 period, the occupations within this group together are projected to *shrink* 4.1%, instead of growing. This is the worst outlook among all major occupation groups.

16. Transportation and Material Moving Occupations

(Median wage: $30,730; 10-year growth: 6.3%)

Counting 7% of the total 156 million workforce in the U.S., workers in the group of transportation and material moving occupations are paid a median wage of $30,730.

Consisting of 52 detailed occupations, this major group includes occupations such as laborers and freight, stock, and material movers, heavy and tractor-trailer truck drivers, light truck or delivery services drivers, packers and packagers, industrial truck and tractor operators, school or special client bus drivers, driver/sales workers, cleaners of vehicles and equipment, first-line supervisors of transportation and material-moving machine and vehicle operators, taxi drivers and chauffeurs, first-line supervisors of helpers, laborers, and material movers, transit and intercity bus drivers, parking lot attendants, refuse and recyclable material collectors, flight attendants, automotive and watercraft service attendants, machine feeders and offbearers, airline pilots, copilots, and flight engineers, excavating and loading machine and dragline operators, crane and tower operators, railroad conductors and yardmasters, locomotive engineers, and commercial pilots.

Average **airline pilots, copilots, and flight engineers** earns a very attractive $127,820 salary annually, the highest within this major group. Average **parking lot attendants** take home $21,730 annually, the lowest within this major group.

Over the 2016 to 2026 period, the occupations within this group together are projected to grow 6.3%, modestly more sluggish than the average growth of 7.4% across all occupations.

17. Healthcare Support Occupations

(Median wage: $27,910; 10-year growth: 23.2%)

Counting only 3% of the total 156 million workforce in the U.S., workers in the group of healthcare support occupations are paid a median wage of $27,910.

This major occupation group consists of only 17 detailed occupations, including nursing assistants, home health aides, medical assistants, dental assistants, phlebotomists, massage therapists, physical therapist assistants, veterinary assistants and laboratory animal caretakers, psychiatric aides, medical transcriptionists, orderlies, medical equipment preparers, physical therapist aides, occupational therapy assistants, pharmacy aides, and occupational therapy aides.

An average **occupational therapy assistant** earns $59,610 annually, the highest within this major group. Average **home health aides** take home $22,660 annually, the lowest within this major group.

Over the 2016 to 2026 period, the occupations within this group together are projected to grow a fabulous 23.2%, leaving in the dust the job growth of any other major occupations groups.

18. Sales and Related Occupations

(Median wage: $26,590; 10-year growth: 3.2%)

Counting 10% of the total 156 million workforce in the U.S., workers in the group of sales and related occupations are paid a median wage of $26,590.

The second largest major occupation group in terms of the number of employees, 14.5 million of them, this group consists of 22 detailed occupations.

These occupations include retail salespersons, cashiers, wholesale and manufacturing sales representatives, first-line supervisors of retail sales workers, counter and rental clerks, insurance sales agents, securities, commodities, and financial services sales agents, first-line supervisors of non-retail sales workers, parts salespersons, telemarketers, real estate sales agents, advertising sales agents, demonstrators and product promoters, sales engineers, travel agents, real estate brokers, gaming change persons and booth cashiers, door-to-door sales workers, news and street vendors, and related workers, and models.

An average **sales engineer** earns $100,000 annually, the highest within this major group. Average **cashiers** take home $20,180 annually, the lowest within this major group.

Over the 2016 to 2026 period, the occupations within this group together are projected to grow 3.2%, less than half of the average growth of 7.4% across all occupations.

19. Building and Grounds Cleaning and Maintenance Occupations

(Median wage: $24,700; 10-year growth: 8.7%)

Counting 4% of the total 156 million workforce in the U.S., workers in the group of building and grounds cleaning and maintenance occupations are paid a median wage of $24,700.

Consisting of only 10 detailed occupations, this group includes the following occupations: Janitors and cleaners, maids and housekeeping cleaners, landscaping and groundskeeping workers, first-line supervisors of housekeeping and janitorial workers, first-line supervisors of landscaping, lawn service, and groundskeeping workers, pest control workers, tree trimmers and pruners, pesticide handlers, sprayers, and applicators, and building cleaning workers.

Average **first-line supervisors of landscaping, lawn service, and grounds keeping workers** earn $45,740 annually, the highest within this major group. Average **maids and housekeeping cleaners** take home $21,820 annually, the lowest within this major group.

Over the 2016 to 2026 period, the occupations within this group together are projected to grow 8.7%, faster than the average growth of 7.4% across all occupations.

20. Farming, Fishing, and Forestry Occupations

(Median wage: $23,510; 10-year growth: 0%)

Counting a miniscule 0.7% of the total 156 million workforce in the U.S., workers in the group of farming, fishing, and forestry occupations are paid a median wage of $23,510.

This is the smallest occupation group employing only 463,000 people, consisting of 14 detailed occupations including farmworkers and laborers, crop, nursery, and greenhouse, agricultural products graders and sorters, farmworkers (farm, ranch, and aquacultural animals), agricultural equipment operators, logging equipment operators, first-line supervisors of farming, fishing, and forestry workers, agricultural inspectors, forest and conservation workers, fallers, log graders and scalers, other logging workers, animal breeders, and fishers and related fishing workers.

Average **supervisors of farming, fishing, and forestry workers** earn $45,320 annually, the highest within this major group. Average **farmworkers and crop, nursery, and greenhouse laborers** take home $22,000 annually, the lowest within this major group.

Over the 2016 to 2026 period, the occupations within this group together are projected to stay flat. Zero growth.

21. Personal Care and Service Occupations

(Median wage: $22,710; 10-year growth: 18.2%)

Counting 4% of the total 156 million workforce in the U.S., workers in the group of personal care and service occupations are paid a median wage of $22,710.

This occupation group consists of 14 detailed occupations including personal care aides, childcare workers, hairdressers, hairstylists, and cosmetologists, recreation workers, amusement and recreation attendants, fitness trainers and aerobics instructors, first-line supervisors of personal service workers, nonfarm animal caretakers, ushers, lobby attendants, and ticket takers, residential advisors, gaming dealers, manicurists and pedicurists, baggage porters and bellhops, skincare specialists, tour guides and escorts, funeral attendants, concierges, morticians, undertakers, and funeral directors, gaming supervisors, locker room, coatroom, and dressing room attendants, barbers, shampooers, entertainment attendants and related workers, and animal trainers.

Average **theatrical and performance makeup artists** earn $60,970 annually, the highest within this major group. Average **gaming dealers** take home $19,290 annually, the lowest within this major group.

Over the 2016 to 2026 period, the occupations within this group together are projected to grow a remarkable 18.2%, two times and a half as briskly as the average growth of 7.4% across all occupations.

22. Food Preparation and Serving Related Occupations

(Median wage: $20,810; 10-year growth: 9.3%)

Counting 9% of the total 156 million workforce in the U.S., workers in the group of food preparation and serving related occupations are paid a median wage of $20,810.

The third largest major occupation group in terms of the number of employees, nearly 13 million of them, this group consists of 18 detailed occupations.

These occupations include combined food preparation and serving workers, waiters and waitresses, restaurant and fast food cooks, first-line supervisors of food preparation and serving workers, food preparation workers, bartenders, dishwashers, counter attendants, cafeteria, food concession, and coffee shop, dining room and cafeteria attendants and bartender helpers, institution and cafeteria cooks, hosts and hostesses, restaurant, lounge, and coffee shop, nonrestaurant food servers, chefs and head cooks, and private household cooks.

Average **supervisors of chefs and head cooks** earn $43,180 annually, the highest within this major group. Average **food preparation and serving workers (including fast food)** take home $19,440 annually, the lowest within this major group.

Over the 2016 to 2026 period, the occupations within this group together are projected to grow 9.3%, faster than the average growth of 7.4% across all occupations.

***

So, here they are, the 22 major occupation groups. For each of us, the line of work we do and will do falls into one of these groups, excluding those falling into the 23rd major group of military specific occupations. Knowing what is out there and how the options stack up against one another helps us make smart choices.

The salaries across these job groups are poles apart. For example, as we have seen above, the management occupations pay a 6-figure median salary of $100,790, nearly five times of that of the food preparation and serving related occupations which is a meager $20,810.

The major occupation groups are broad groups, each containing a variety of lines of work that require different levels of education and skillsets, and are subject to vastly different levels of supply and demand in the labor market.

As a result, even within the same major group, the

median wages associated with the occupations are no less different than the median wages across major groups.

For instance, within the major group of healthcare practitioners and technical occupations, anesthesiologists enjoy a dazzling median salary of $247,339 which is more than 9 times of that of dietetic technicians ($26,350) in the same group.

Therefore, even if we have our eyes set in a particular broad line of work, we still need to be informed of variations within the broad line of work, for us to make wise career decisions.

In addition to salary variation, the growth outlook of the 22 occupation groups is also highly disparate. While the healthcare support occupations group is projected to grow a wonderful 23.2%, the production occupations group is forecasted to shrink a depressing 4.1%, over the same 10-year period of 2016 to 2026.

In the next chapter, we will identify a deciding factor that is responsible for the enormous disparity in salary and growth outlook: Education.

3 SECRET SAUCE TO GREAT JOBS

An investment in knowledge always pays the best interest.

— Benjamin Franklin, The Way to Wealth

There are no other thoughtful quotes more fitting than the above from what Benjamin Franklin, one of the Founding Fathers of the United States, wrote in his book *The Way to Wealth*.

The best way to acquire knowledge and garner its power is through education. For the purposes of this book, we will see in this chapter that education plays an enormous role in differentiating between occupations, in terms of salary and growth outlook.

As seen in previous chapters, occupations are vastly different in salary and future growth prospects. Some occupations pay top dollars, some are projected to grow substantially in future, while others pay only a fraction of what would be considered to be a good salary or do not enjoy promising future growth prospects.

Take computer and information systems managers for example. Computer and information systems managers are typically paid a first-rate annual salary of $135,800 across the country, and the demand for these jobs is forecasted to grow at a rapid pace of 11.9% from 2016 to 2026, much faster than the all-occupation average growth of 7.4%. This looks a great occupation.

In contrast, while airline pilots, copilots, and flight engineers typically make also a similarly attractive annual salary of $127,820 to that of the computer and information systems managers, the demand for this occupation will grow only a sluggish 3.4% between 2016 and 2026.

As another example, let us take a look at home health aides who help people with disabilities, chronic illnesses, or cognitive impairment by assisting in their daily living activities.

Although home health aides jobs are projected to grow a blistering 46.7%, they are paid a teeny annual salary of $22,600, only a tiny fraction of top salaries paid in other occupations.

We have to ask: Why? What are the underlying reasons that drive all these differences?

Supply and Demand Are the Answer

The answer lies in the balance between supply and demand of individual occupations in the labor market, a key driving factor that determines largely an occupation's wage level and future outlook.

Some occupations are in high demand, relative to the supply, and thus pay out lucrative salaries and have a bright outlook. Other occupations have low demand, again relative to the supply, and thus pay only low wages and have a gloomy prospect.

In the 21st century, some occupations naturally have larger demand than others. For instance, software developers outnumber farmers easily, due to the structure of modern economy which saw rapid proliferation of a variety of computing devices.

As a result, software developers are needed in a much larger quantity than farmers are. Consequently, software developers earn more than farmers.

Therefore, we see that the structure, composition, and trend of an economy determine the demand for an occupation. Industries that are driven by newer technologies and emerging trend of demographics benefit from greater demand in future years.

For example, solar photovoltaic installers and wind turbine service technicians are projected to grow a phenomenal 105% and 96% from 2016 to 2026, respectively, both clear winners thanks to the technology trend of the energy sector switching from traditional fossil fuel to alternative energy sources including solar and wind energy.

An increasingly aging population in the U.S. is an ongoing demographic trend that drives vigorous demand for the healthcare practitioners and technical occupations, as well as healthcare support occupations.

On the flip side, manufacturing jobs are projected to further decline in the future due to continued outsourcing of the manufacturing industries to cheaper regions of the globe.

After making the above observations, it is tempting to conclude that high demand occupations are good jobs that pay decently. However, demand alone does not tell the whole story.

Recall the home health aides example earlier who are projected to grow substantially, signifying high demand for the occupation, but the median salary is very small.

Another example. Comparing to software developers, we have far fewer anesthesiologists than software developers, but anesthesiologists are paid much more. Why? Is not the demand for software developers greater than that for anesthesiologists?

True. Society needs a lot more software developers than anesthesiologists. But on the other side, the supply side, our society produces far fewer anesthesiologists than software developers.

On the one hand, it generally takes only a four-year undergraduate degree to become a software developer. On the other hand, to become an anesthesiologist, it takes four years in undergraduate study, four years in a medical school, plus three years internship or residency, for a total of eleven years.

Only a handful of us are willing and able to invest eleven years in order to become an anesthesiologist, a major reason why our society produces only a handful anesthesiologists each year.

Although software developers win on the demand side, anesthesiologists win on the supply side. Thus, the relative demand (relative to supply of course), but not the absolute demand, is the deciding factor in terms of job wage and growth prospect.

With this understanding, we should look for occupations that have strong demand relative to supply.

Which direction should we look?

The comparison above between software developers and anesthesiologists provides a crucial hint. The hint is that as an occupation requires more and more years of education and training, the demand for the occupation becomes smaller than the demand for occupations requiring only simpler skillsets.

However, the supply of qualified workers drops even more so than does the demand.

This creates supply and demand imbalance, with insufficient supply to meet demand, therefore increasing the value of the workers in the occupation. As a result, the workers are paid more.

Therefore, it becomes empirically clear that education requirement of an occupation is perhaps an influential factor, maybe the most influential factor, that tilts the occupation's supply and demand in favor of us, if we are willing and able to attain high level of education.

This is a key observation that we are making. While the economy structure and the trend of demographics are key, too, they are out of our control as individuals, as we cannot simply will the trend to go the direction of our wish.

But, education is under our control. We decide whether, when, and how to pursue education, and in what field. It is not exaggerating to say that our education level is the factor under our control that has the largest impact on what kind of jobs we will have, how much we will earn at the job, and how safe our job will be in future.

In the U.S., the options for education are wide ranging.

Beyond high school, there are more than 7,000 postsecondary institutions, and around 4,700 of them are 2-year or 4-year degree granting colleges. Beyond Bachelor's degree, there are plenty of options of obtaining a Master's, doctoral, or professional degree.

Here is a list of education levels we can achieve in the U.S. These are the official categorization of education attainment levels in the employment data released by the U.S. Department of Labor:

- No formal educational credential

- High school diploma or equivalent

- Some college, no degree

- Postsecondary nondegree award

- Associate's degree

- Bachelor's degree

- Master's degree

- Doctoral or professional degree.

In the remainder of the chapter, let us take a close look at these education levels in details, and focus on comparing the typical wages paid at each level.

For us to get a sense of how much salary each education

level earns, let us remind ourselves of the wage that an average worker makes in the U.S., $37,040. We will be comparing constantly to this national median wage across all occupations.

No Formal Educational Credential

(Median Wage: $22,410)

Can you believe it? In the 156 million workforce in the United States of America, the most developed country in the world and the largest economy in the world, there are 37 million, or 24% of the 156 million, who do not have a formal educational credentials. That is nearly a quarter of the workforce.

The occupations in this category typically do not require a formal credential issued by an educational institution, such as a high school diploma or postsecondary certificate, for entry into the occupation.

Examples of occupations in this category include janitors and cleaners, cashiers, and agricultural equipment operators.

Of course, it is no surprise that a typical worker in these occupations makes far less, $22,410, than the all-occupation median wage of $37,040.

If we find ourselves falling into this category of education (or a lack of it), of course one way to get out of this situation is to pursue more education or training: Get a certificate or a degree. This will improve greatly our chances of moving on to a higher paying occupation.

If, however, for whatever reason, we are unable to pursue further education, what can we do? No worries, it's not the end of the world. Even without formal educational credentials, there are occupations that we can go into and get paid far more than the median wage of $22,410 in this category.

Among the occupations whose entry positions do not require a formal educational credential, the top 10 highest paying jobs are listed in the following:

1. Artists and related workers: $61,360 (median wage)

2. Mine shuttle car operators: $56,450 (median wage)

3. Rotary drill operators, oil and gas: $54,430 (median wage)

4. Loading machine operators, underground mining: $53,420 (median wage)

5. Continuous mining machine operators: $51,840 (median wage)

6. Tapers: $48,990 (median wage)

7. Service unit operators, oil, gas, and mining: $48,610 (median wage)

8. Derrick operators, oil and gas: $48,130 (median wage)

9. Athletes and sports competitors: $47,710 (median wage)

10. Hoist and winch operators: $42,530 (median wage).

Without a formal education credential, we can be an artist or an athlete and make a decent wage. An average artist (#1 above) takes home $61,360, while an average athlete earns $42,530.

If we are not really artist or athlete material, going into oil, gas and mining related occupations seems a good choice. These occupations in the list above all make way above $22,410. In fact, any of the 10 jobs above pays a median wage significantly higher than the all-occupation median wage of $37,040. Not bad at all.

Let us now move on to the next education level.

High School Diploma or Equivalent

(Median Wage: $35,540)

There are 62 million workers who have only a high school diploma or equivalent but have no further education or training beyond this. These 62 million workers are roughly 39% of the total workforce of 156 million in the U.S.

This category indicates the completion of high school or an equivalent program resulting in the award of a high school diploma or an equivalent, such as the General Education Development (GED) credential.

Examples of occupations in this category include social and human service assistants, carpenters, and pharmacy technicians.

An average worker with this level of education attainment takes home $35,540, slightly less than but close to the all-occupation median wage of $37,040.

It does not seem hard to make close to the all-occupation median wage. It takes only a high school diploma or equivalent. It takes only 12 years after kindergarten.

As seen previously, workers with no formal educational credential make up 24% of the total workforce, while those with only a high school diploma or equivalent make up 39% of the total workforce. So together these two categories make up 63% of the total workforce.

If we have successfully graduated from high school, congratulations to ourselves! Roughly, we are already doing as fine as a considerable portion of the U.S. workforce, at least in terms of the wage income we can take home, even if we are just an average worker but not a workplace superstar.

If we have only a high school diploma or equivalent, we

can still be smart about deciding which occupation to take. Among the occupations whose entry positions require only high school diploma or equivalent, the top 10 highest paying jobs are listed in the following:

1. Nuclear power reactor operators: $91,170 (median wage)

2. Transportation, storage, and distribution managers: $89,190 (median wage)

3. First-line supervisors of police and detectives: $84,840 (median wage)

4. Power distributors and dispatchers: $81,900 (median wage)

5. Elevator installers and repairers: $78,890 (median wage)

6. Detectives and criminal investigators: $78,120 (median wage)

7. Commercial pilots: $77,200 (median wage)

8. Media and communication equipment workers, all other: $75,700 (median wage)

9. Power plant operators: $74,690 (median wage)

10. First-line supervisors of non-retail sales workers: $73,150 (median wage).

First thing to notice about the above top 10 highest paying jobs is that any of them pays about twice or more of the all-occupation median wage. It is truly encouraging, and amazing at the same time, that even with a high school diploma, there are jobs out there that pay really really well.

For example, the nuclear power reactor operators (#1) take home an outstanding median wage of $91,170, way more than the all-occupation median wage of $37,040. Another example: First-line supervisors of non-retail sales workers (#10) make a very nice median wage of $73,150.

Some College but No Degree

(Median Wage: $34,520)

This category signifies the achievement of a high school diploma or equivalent plus the completion of one or more postsecondary courses that did not result in a degree or award.

There are about 4 million workers in this category, only 3% of the total U.S. workforce of 156 million. An average worker in the category makes $34,520, slightly less than the all-occupation median wage of $37,040.

An example of an occupation in this category is actors. Of course, if you make it on the big screen or on the TV screen and become famous, you probably will make 100 times of $34,520, or more.

For those of us who were not born with a lot of acting talent, there are still non-acting jobs that come with decent salaries. Below are the only 5 occupations that we can get into with only some college but no degree, among the 820 occupations in the U.S. Department of Labor data:

1. Actors: median wage data not available

2. Computer user support specialists: $49,390 (median wage)

3. Bookkeeping, accounting, and auditing clerks: $38,390 (median wage)

4. Computer, automated teller, and office machine repairers: $37,100 (median wage)

5. Teacher assistants: $25,410 (median wage).

While it does not seem that we would have a lot of occupational choices with only some college education but no degree, 3 out of the 5 such jobs pay at or above the all-occupation median wage.

However, if this level of pay does not satisfy you, get more education! Read on to find out how much additional education pays off.

Postsecondary Nondegree Award

(Median Wage: $36,860)

These programs lead to a certificate or other award, but not a degree. The certificate is awarded by the educational institution and is the result of completing formal postsecondary schooling.

Note that certification, issued by a professional organization or certifying body, is not included here.

Some postsecondary nondegree award programs last only a few weeks, while others may last 1 to 2 years.

Examples of occupations in this category include nursing assistants, emergency medical technicians (EMT's) and paramedics, and hairstylists.

There are about 10 million workers in this category, only 6% of the total U.S. workforce of 156 million. An average worker in the category makes $36,860, slightly less than the all-occupation median wage of $37,040.

Among the occupations whose entry positions require only a postsecondary nondegree award, the top 10 highest paying jobs are listed in the following:

1. Powerhouse, substation, and relay electrical and electronics repairers: $75,670 (median wage)

2. First-line supervisors of fire-fighting and prevention workers: $74,540 (median wage)

3. Captains, mates, and pilots of water vessels: $72,680

(median wage)

4. Ship engineers: $70,570 (median wage)

5. Insurance appraisers, auto damage: $63,510 (median wage)

6. Makeup artists, theatrical and performance: $60,970 (median wage)

7. Aircraft mechanics and service technicians: $60,170 (median wage)

8. Electrical and electronics installers and repairers, transportation equipment: $59,280 (median wage)

9. Fire inspectors and investigators: $58,440 (median wage)

10. Commercial and industrial equipment electrical and electronics repairers: $56,250 (median wage).

All of the 10 jobs here pay much more than the all-occupation median wage of $37,040, with powerhouse electrical and electronics repairers (#1) paid twice of that amount at $75,670. However, commercial and industrial equipment electrical and electronics repairers (#10) are paid at only $56,250. Pay attention to subtle differences and choose wisely.

Associate's Degree

(Median Wage: $51,270)

Completion of an Associate's degree usually requires at least 2 years but not more than 4 years of full-time academic study beyond high school.

Examples of occupations in this category include mechanical drafters, respiratory therapists, and dental hygienists.

There are about 4 million workers in this category, only 2% of the total U.S. workforce of 156 million. An average worker in the category makes $51,270, far higher than the all-occupation median wage of $37,040.

It takes only 2 years beyond high school to get an Associate's degree and leave the all-occupation median wage of $37,040 behind in the dust.

Among the occupations whose entry positions require only an Associate's degree, the median pays vary widely, with the top 10 highest paying jobs listed in the following:

1. Air traffic controllers: $122,410 (median wage)

2. Radiation therapists: $80,160 (median wage)

3. Nuclear technicians: $79,140 (median wage)

4. Nuclear medicine technologists: $74,350 (median wage)

5. Funeral service managers: $73,830 (median wage)

6. Dental hygienists: $72,910 (median wage)

7. Diagnostic medical sonographers: $69,650 (median wage)

8. Magnetic resonance imaging technologists: $68,420 (median wage)

9. Aerospace engineering and operations technicians: $68,020 (median wage)

10. Web developers: $66,130 (median wage).

With only an Associate's degree, air traffic controllers (#1) take home a stellar 6-figure salary of $122,410. Even the last one on the top-10 list, web developers, take home a median wage much higher than the all-occupation median wage of $37,040.

Bachelor's Degree

(Median Wage: $71,550)

Completion of a Bachelor's degree generally requires at least 4 years, but not more than 5 years, of full-time academic study beyond high school.

Examples of occupations in this category include budget analysts, dietitians and nutritionists, and civil engineers, among many others.

There are about 33 million workers in this category, about 21% of the total U.S. workforce of 156 million. An average worker in the category makes $71,550, almost twice as high as the all-occupation median wage of $37,040.

It takes only 4 years beyond high school to get an Bachelor's degree and double the take-home wage that a high school graduate makes.

The workforce in this category is the classical American middle class, with a college degree, a decent wage income, and a comfortable lifestyle.

Among the occupations whose entry positions require a Bachelor's degree, the median salaries vary widely, with the top 10 highest paying jobs listed in the following:

1. Chief executives: $181,210 (median wage)

2. Computer and information systems managers: $135,800 (median wage)

3. Architectural and engineering managers: $134,730 (median wage)

4. Marketing managers: $131,180 (median wage)

5. Petroleum engineers: $128,230 (median wage)

6. Airline pilots, copilots, and flight engineers: $127,820 (median wage)

7.   Financial managers: $121,750 (median wage)

8.   Natural sciences managers: $119,850 (median wage)

9.   Sales managers: $117,960 (median wage)

10. Compensation and benefits managers: $116,240 (median wage).

With a college degree, the door of opportunities afforded in the U.S. is all of a sudden wide open to us. Take a good look at the top-10 list above, and realize for ourselves how fast education pays off itself.

The list contains a wide range of different lines of work, including corporate senior-most management jobs, chief executives. Even a mediocre chief executive takes home a superb $181,210, nearly 5 times of the all-occupation median wage.

All of the jobs on the list pay a 6-figure median salary, with the last one on the list, compensation and benefits managers, earns an impressive 6-figure of $116,240.

Master's Degree

(Median Wage: $68,090)

Completion of a Master's degree usually requires 1 or 2 years of full-time academic study beyond a Bachelor's degree.

Examples of occupations in this category include statisticians, physician assistants, and educational, guidance, school, and vocational counselors.

There are about 3 million workers in this category, only 2% of the total U.S. workforce of 156 million. Not too many people possess a highest degree of a Master's. People usually either stop at a Bachelor's degree, or move on beyond a Master's to obtain a doctoral degree.

An average worker in the category makes $68,090, far more than the all-occupation median wage of $37,040.

But the median wage of $68,090 is lower than that of the Bachelor's degree. This is puzzling. It seems like a couple low paying occupations in this category dragged down the median wage of the whole category.

These low paying occupations are rehabilitation counselors with a median wage of only $34,670 and mental health counselors with a median wage of $42,840.

Among the occupations whose entry positions require typically a Master's degree, the top 10 highest paying jobs are listed in the following:

1. Nurse anesthetists: $160,270 (median wage)

2. Political scientists: $114,290 (median wage)

3. Computer and information research scientists:

$111,840 (median wage)

4. Mathematicians: $105,810 (median wage)

5. Physician assistants: $101,480 (median wage)

6. Economists: $101,050 (median wage)

7. Nurse practitioners: $100,910 (median wage)

8. Nurse midwives: $99,770 (median wage)

9. Psychologists, all other: $95,710 (median wage)

10. Education administrators, elementary and secondary school: $92,510 (median wage).

Among the top-10 list, nurse anesthetists (#1) make the most at $160,270, followed by political scientists paid a median salary of $114,290. There are 2 other nurse jobs on this list: Nurse practitioners (#7) with a median salary of $100,910 and nurse midwives (#8) with a median pay of $99,770.

Doctoral or Professional Degree

(Median Wage: $102,230)

This is the highest level of education attainment. Completion of a doctoral degree (Ph.D.) usually requires at least 3 years of full-time academic work beyond a Bachelor's degree. Completion of a professional degree usually requires at least 3 years of full-time academic study beyond a Bachelor's degree.

Examples of occupations for which a doctoral or professional degree is the typical form of entry-level education include lawyers, physicists, and dentists.

There are about 4 million workers in this category, only 3% of the total U.S. workforce of 156 million. Jobs requiring a doctoral degree or a professional degree to get in pay extremely well. An average worker in the category makes $102,230, almost three times of the all-occupation median wage of $37,040.

Among these occupations, the salaries vary widely, with the top 10 highest paying jobs listed in the following:

1. Anesthesiologists: $247,339 (median wage)

2. Surgeons: $232,028 (median wage)

3. Obstetricians and gynecologists: $214,963 (median wage)

4. Oral and maxillofacial surgeons: $213,642 (median wage)

5. Orthodontists: $209,890 (median wage)

6. Physicians and surgeons, all other: $206,920 (median wage)

7. Internists, general: $196,380 (median wage)

8. Psychiatrists: $194,740 (median wage)

9. Family and general practitioners: $190,490 (median wage)

10. Dentists, all other specialists: $173,000 (median wage).

Many of the jobs in the top-10 list are also ranked very high on the top 100 highest paying occupations across all lines of work and across all education attainment levels, as we will see in a later chapter.

All of the jobs on the list here are healthcare practitioner jobs typically requiring professional degrees, with anesthesiologists topping the list with a breathtaking median salary of $247,339.

How do non-healthcare occupations do? Excluding all healthcare occupations, the following 10 jobs requiring typically a doctoral or professional degree also pay top dollars:

1. Judges, magistrate judges, and magistrates: $125,880 (median wage)

2. Lawyers: $118,160 (median wage)

3. Physicists: $115,870 (median wage)

4. Computer and information research scientists: $111,840 (median wage)

5. Law teachers, postsecondary: $111,210 (median wage)

6. Astronomers: $104,740 (median wage)

7. Health specialties teachers, postsecondary: $99,360 (median wage)

8. Engineering teachers, postsecondary: $97,530 (median wage)

9. Economics teachers, postsecondary: $95,770 (median wage)

10. Administrative law judges, adjudicators, and hearing officers: $92,110 (median wage).

Out of these 10 jobs, 4 are lawyers and judges in the legal world: Judges (#1) with a median salary of $125,880, lawyers (#2) with a median salary of $118,160, postsecondary law teachers (#5) with a median salary of $111,210, and administrative law judges with a median salary of $92,110.

Out of these 10 jobs, 4 are postsecondary teacher jobs: Postsecondary law teachers (#5) with a median wage of $111,210, health specialties teachers (#7) with a median salary of $99,360, engineering teachers (#8) with a median wage of $97,530, and economics teachers (#9) with a median wage of $95,770.

Half of these 10 jobs are science, technology and engineering jobs: The natural science job of physicists (#2) with a median salary of $115,870, computer and information research scientists (#4) with a median salary of $111,840, astronomers (#6) with a median salary of $104,740, engineering teachers (#8) with a median salary of $97,530, and the social science job of economics teachers (#9) with a median salary of $95,770.

Based on what we have seen above, it is clear that among the top echelons in the U.S. workforce, in terms of salary incomes and education credentials, healthcare practitioners sit atop squarely, followed by legal occupations of lawyers and judges, postsecondary teachers, and then science, technology and engineering jobs.

Education and Wage

Now we have examined all the education attainment levels in the U.S. and the typical wages earned at these levels, the pattern has emerged indisputably that the typical salary paid in an occupation is strongly connected to the education level required for the occupation.

Using the median salary across all occupations as a yardstick, Figure 3 below illustrates vividly the comparison between typical salaries that we have seen above across education levels.

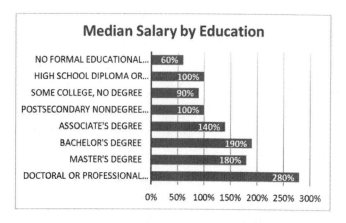

Figure 3. Median Salary by Education

The percentages in the figure are relative to the all-occupation median wage of $37,040, represented by the 100% vertical line. Among the 8 education attainment levels, half of them earn less than this median wage or at this level.

If we have no formal education credentials at all, not even a high school diploma, we will be typically making a salary of $22,410, only 60% of $37,040.

For those of us who have either a high school diploma or equivalent, some college but no degree, or postsecondary nondegree award (read certificate), we will be making an annual salary of $35,540, $34,520, and $36,860, respectively, all roughly on a par with $37,040.

Beyond these 4 education attainment levels, the remaining 4 levels make far more than the all-occupation median salary of $37,040.

With an Associate's degree, we can make a typical salary of $51,270 which is 140% of the all-occupation median.

With a Bachelor's degree or a Master's degree, our typical salary would be $71,550, 190% of the all-occupation median salary of $37,040, almost doubled.

With a Master's degree, our typical salary would be $68,090 which is 180% of the all-occupation median salary of $37,040.

The top median is awarded to some of us who are willing and able to pursue the highest education level to put a doctorate or a professional degree under our belt. With this achievement, the typical salary is $102,230 which is 280% of the all-occupation median, nearly tripled.

Education and Unemployment Rate

In the labor market, the value of education is not only recognized in better salaries but also reflected in lower unemployment rates.

Figure 4 below shows a comparison of unemployment rates in 2016 among workers age 25 and above who are grouped according to their education attainment levels.

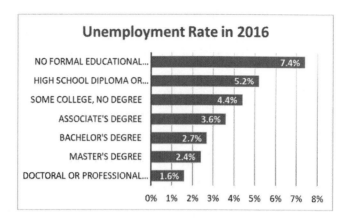

Figure 4. Unemployment Rate by Education

While the overall unemployment rate across all education attainment levels was 4% in 2016, the unemployment rate shows clear differentiation by education level.

The following three groups suffered unemployment rates higher than the average 4%.

The group of workers who have no formal educational credentials had the highest unemployment rate of 7.4%, followed by the group having a high school diploma or equivalent who had an unemployment rate of 5.2%.

Workers who have some college education but did not obtain a degree had an unemployment rate of 4.4%.

The remaining four groups enjoyed unemployment rates lower than the average 4%.

In particular, the unemployment rate for workers with

an Associate's degree was 3.6%. It was 2.7% for Bachelor's degree holders, and 2.4% for Master's degree holders.

At the top education level of doctoral or professional degree holders, the unemployment rate was only 1.6%, much lower than the average 4%.

Education and Job Growth Outlook

In addition to salary and unemployment rate disparities, growth of the number of available jobs also differs greatly by the level of education attainment.

Figure 5 below demonstrates a comparison of job growth from 2016 to 2026 by typical entry-level education.

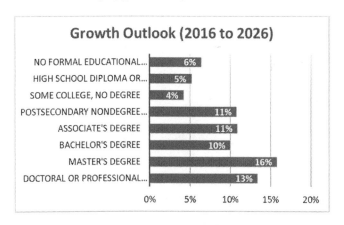

Figure 5. Job Growth Outlook by Education

Recall between 2016 and 2026, the overall number of jobs available in the U.S. is projected to grow 7.4%. From Figure 5, it is clear that lower levels of education attainment, including no formal education credentials, high school diploma or equivalent, and some college but no degree, are projected to have job growth below the average growth of 7.4%.

Higher levels of education attainment are forecasted to have greater growth in job availability. In particular, jobs typically requiring a Master's degree for entry-level positions enjoy the greatest growth of 16%, more than twice of the average growth of 7.4%.

Jobs typically requiring a doctoral or professional degree for entry-level positions are projected to grow 13%, nearly twice as much as the average growth of 7.4%.

Occupations typically requiring a Bachelor's degree, an Associate's degree, or some kind of postsecondary nondegree award for entry-level positions are projected to grow between 10% and 11%, much faster than the average growth of 7.4%.

***

The analyses above clearly show that education helps us obtain a job that pays well and at the same time is secure, without as much worry of losing the job as otherwise.

When buying a home, our real estate agents always remind us of the saying "location, location, location", speaking to the supreme importance of location in the value of a home.

In examining the earning potential, unemployment rates, and job growth outlook above, three highly important consideration factors when we choose an occupation, the point we are making here is clearly "education, education, education".

There is no ambiguity of the utter importance of education in the real employment data we just analyzed in this chapter.

Each level of education we complete may help us develop additional skills, give us access to higher paying occupations, and signal that we are able to follow through on important tasks, such as planning ahead and meeting deadlines, that employers value.

Go pursue an education level that you are able to achieve and can afford, as high as possible. This is the surest bet, the biggest bang for the buck (and the time and effort you spend), to land a secure job that pays well. Also, remember that if a job pays well, usually it is safe job, too.

However, if, for whatever reason, we are stuck at a certain level of education, and we cannot afford or do not have opportunities to pursue further education, there is no reason to panic.

We have seen previously in this chapter that for a given education attainment level, there are occupations that are paying far higher than other occupations. Thus, we just need to be informed and be cognizant about this salary variation, and pick an occupation that pays a decent salary, without having to moving up on the educational ladder.

Knowledge is power and is certainly fortune, too.

4 MAPPING OUT A CAREER

We keep moving forward, opening new doors, and doing new things, because we're curious and curiosity keeps leading us down new paths.

— *Walt Disney*

In the United States of America, among the 50 states and Washington, D.C., jobs are obviously not distributed evenly. The number of jobs, types of jobs and salaries that the jobs pay vary greatly between the states and Washington, D.C., due to their population, geographical location which is key to commerce, level of economic development, and concentration of certain industries.

Many of us want to stay close to our families and friends, are used to the communities in which we grew up, or simply find going to unfamiliar places too stressful. In these cases, finding a local job would be our first choice.

There are also many of us who think differently in this perspective. We find local life not exciting anymore and instead long for further exploring life in a new place. For those of us, finding a job in a faraway place would be ideal.

Regardless of the location preferences we have, learning the differences in the jobs that the 50 states and Washington, D.C., offer enables us to examine the choices that we are to make in a rational way, important in making an informed career decision most suitable to our individual needs.

In this chapter, let us find out how employment opportunities differ across the 50 states and Washington, D.C. In addition, we will also find out the top metropolitan areas in the U.S. that provide the best job opportunities.

Jobs and States

Below we list out the number of jobs by state (including Washington, D.C.), in a descending order. The median salary for the jobs in each state is also provided in the parentheses.

Number 1 to 10 States

1. California: 16.0 million jobs ($40,920)

2. Texas: 11.7 million jobs ($35,480)

3. New York: 9.1 million jobs ($42,760)

4. Florida: 8.2 million jobs ($32,790)

5. Illinois: 5.9 million jobs ($38,270)

6. Pennsylvania: 5.7 million jobs ($36,680)

7. Ohio: 5.3 million jobs ($35,760)

8. North Carolina: 4.2 million jobs ($33,920)

9. Georgia: 4.2 million jobs ($34,330)

10. Michigan: 4.2 million jobs ($36,030)

California and Texas are the only two states in America that each offers more than 10 million jobs. California has 16 million jobs, accounting for 11% of all jobs in the U.S.

This means that 1 in every 9 jobs are in California. The Golden State. Rightly so! The median wage of California jobs is $40,920, 10% higher than the national median salary of $37,040.

Texas has nearly 12 million jobs, representing 8% of all jobs in the U.S. This means 1 in 12 jobs are in Texas. The median salary of Texas jobs is $35,480, slightly lower than the national median. However, Texas does not levy a state tax which makes a positive difference in terms of the after-tax income.

New York's 9 million jobs is ranked #3. On the one hand, the New York's median salary of $42,760 is in fact the highest among the top-10 list above. On the other hand, it is no secret that the living expense in New York is significantly higher than the national average.

In total, the top 10 states above offer 75 million jobs, counting more than half (53%) of all jobs in the U.S.

Number 11 to 20 States

11. New Jersey: 4.0 million jobs ($41,950)

12. Virginia: 3.8 million jobs ($39,070)

13. Massachusetts: 3.5 million jobs ($46,690)

14. Washington: 3.1 million jobs ($43,400)

15. Indiana: 3.0 million jobs ($33,790)

16. Tennessee: 2.9 million jobs ($32,800)

17. Minnesota: 2.8 million jobs ($40,100)

18. Wisconsin: 2.8 million jobs ($36,250)

19. Missouri: 2.8 million jobs ($34,230)

20. Arizona: 2.7 million jobs ($35,470)

Ranked between #11 and #20 in terms of the number of jobs, these states together offer 31 million jobs, accounting for 22% of all jobs in the U.S.

While Massachusetts boasts a median salary of $46,690, an impressive 26% above the national median salary, Tennessee in this group of states has a median salary of only $32,800, 11% lower than the national median.

It is worth noting that the top 20 states above offer 75% of all jobs in the United States. The remaining 25% of U.S. jobs are spread across the other 30 states and Washington, D.C.

Number 21 to 30 States

21. Maryland: 2.6 million jobs ($43,010)

22. Colorado: 2.5 million jobs ($39,710)

23. South Carolina: 2.0 million jobs ($32,140)

24. Louisiana: 1.9 million jobs ($32,080)

25. Alabama: 1.9 million jobs ($32,100)

26. Kentucky: 1.9 million jobs ($33,190)

27. Oregon: 1.8 million jobs ($37,990)

28. Connecticut: 1.7 million jobs ($45,090)

29. Oklahoma: 1.6 million jobs ($33,140)

30. Iowa: 1.5 million jobs ($34,790)

These states rank between #21 and #30 in terms of the

number of jobs. Together they offer 19 million jobs, accounting for 14% of all jobs in the U.S.

Four out of the 10 states in this group boast median salaries higher than the national median, including Maryland (#21, $43,010), Colorado (#22, $39,710), Oregon (#27, $37,990), and Connecticut (#28, $45,090).

Altogether, the 30 states above account for 89% of all U.S. jobs.

Number 31 to 40 States (and Washington, D.C.)

31. Utah: 1.4 million jobs ($35,010)

32. Kansas: 1.4 million jobs ($34,460)

33. Nevada: 1.3 million jobs ($34,510)

34. Arkansas: 1.2 million jobs ($30,130)

35. Mississippi: 1.1 million jobs ($29,590)

36. Nebraska: 1.0 million jobs ($34,890)

37. New Mexico: 0.8 million jobs ($32,900)

38. District of Columbia: 0.7 million jobs ($67,870)

39. West Virginia: 0.7 million jobs ($30,760)

40. Idaho: 0.7 million jobs ($32,800)

These 10 states rank between #31 and #40 in terms of the number of jobs. Together they offer 10 million jobs, accounting for 7% of all jobs in the U.S.

Nebraska (#36) is the last state boasting 1 million plus jobs, while all other states and Washington D.C. on the remainder of the list each offers less than 1 million jobs.

Although Washington, D.C. (#38) has only 700 thousand jobs, their median salary of $67,870 is higher than any of the 50 states and much higher than the national median salary.

Number 41 to 51 States

41. New Hampshire: 0.6 million jobs ($38,270)

42. Hawaii: 0.6 million jobs ($40,030)

43. Maine: 0.6 million jobs ($35,380)

44. Rhode Island: 0.5 million jobs ($39,730)

45. Montana: 0.5 million jobs ($32,750)

46. Delaware: 0.4 million jobs ($37,960)

47. North Dakota: 0.4 million jobs ($39,160)

48. South Dakota: 0.4 million jobs ($31,590)

49. Alaska: 0.3 million jobs ($47,170)

50. Vermont: 0.3 million jobs ($37,920)

51. Wyoming: 0.3 million jobs ($38,710)

The last 11 states ranking between #41 and #51 on the list together offer 5 million jobs, accounting for a tiny 4% of all jobs in the U.S.

Now we have examined all the 50 states and Washington, D.C. The data clearly demonstrates that the jobs are concentrated in populous states, such as California, Texas, New York, and Florida.

In fact, the top 10 states above account for more than half of all U.S. jobs, much more than small states. This is consistent with common perception.

Ten Highest Paying States

In the above analysis, the 50 states and Washington, D.C., are ranked by the number of the jobs they offer. If, instead, we rank the states and the District of Columbia by the median salary, it is going to be a different picture.

Below we list out the top 10 states and DC, ranked now by their median salary:

1. District of Columbia: 0.7 million jobs ($67,870)

2. Alaska: 0.3 million jobs ($47,170)

3. Massachusetts: 3.5 million jobs ($46,690)

4. Connecticut: 1.7 million jobs ($45,090)

5. Washington: 3.1 million jobs ($43,400)

6. Maryland: 2.6 million jobs ($43,010)

7. New York: 9.1 million jobs ($42,760)

8. New Jersey: 4.0 million jobs ($41,950)

9. California: 16.0 million jobs ($40,920)

10. Minnesota: 2.8 million jobs ($40,100).

All the top 10 on the list have a median salary above the national median of $37,040. Among them, Washington D.C. leads the pack with a median wage that is 183% of the national median.

The states of New York and California not only have many jobs to offer but also take the #7 and #9 spots in terms of the median salary ranking among all the states and Washington D.C.

Together, these top 9 states and Washington, D.C. offer 44 million jobs, accounting for nearly one third (32%) of all U.S. jobs.

For those of us who are open to relocate to a different state for a well-paying job, these top 9 states and Washington, D.C. should be high on our list of candidate locations.

Jobs and Metropolitan Areas

Now let us turn to metropolitan areas in the U.S. and find out about how job opportunities in these metropolises differ.

In the United States, a metropolitan statistical area (MSA) is a geographical region with a relatively high population density at its core and close economic ties throughout the area.

A typical metropolitan area is centered on a single large city that wields substantial influence over the region. For example, Chicago or Atlanta are typical of this type of metropolitan areas.

However, some metropolitan areas contain more than one large city with no single municipality holding a substantially dominant position. Dallas–Fort Worth metroplex, Norfolk-Virginia Beach, Riverside–San Bernardino or Minneapolis–Saint Paul are such examples.

There are in total around 400 such metropolitan areas in the United States. Due to this large number, we will not examine each of them here, as otherwise it would take too much space in this book.

Among them, 35 metropolitan areas offer over 1 million jobs. We instead analyze these 35 metropolitan areas below, ranked by the number of jobs in each area, in a descending order.

The median salary for the jobs in each state is also

provided in the parentheses in each list item below.

Number 1 to 10 Metropolitan Areas

1. New York-Jersey City-White Plains, NY-NJ: 6.6 million jobs ($46,040)

2. Los Angeles-Long Beach-Glendale, CA: 4.2 million jobs ($39,570)

3. Chicago-Naperville-Arlington Heights, IL: 3.6 million jobs ($40,170)

4. Houston-The Woodlands-Sugar Land, TX: 2.9 million jobs ($38,470)

5. Atlanta-Sandy Springs-Roswell, GA: 2.6 million jobs ($37,310)

6. Washington-Arlington-Alexandria, DC-VA-MD-WV: 2.5 million jobs ($53,140)

7. Dallas-Plano-Irving, TX: 2.4 million jobs ($38,400)

8. Phoenix-Mesa-Scottsdale, AZ: 1.9 million jobs ($36,390)

9. Minneapolis-St. Paul-Bloomington, MN-WI: 1.9 million jobs ($43,170)

10. Boston-Cambridge-Newton, MA: 1.8 million jobs ($52,770)

The New York-Jersey City-White Plains area is home to nearly 11 million residents, offering 6.6 million jobs. If this area was a state, it would be ranked #5 among all the states, in terms of the number of jobs that it provides to its population. The jobs in this area boasts a median salary of $46,040, 24% above the national median salary.

Texas is the only state that sports two spots on the top-10 list: The Houston-The Woodlands-Sugar Land (#4) and Dallas-Plano-Irving (#5) areas. Together, these two areas are home to 5.4 million jobs, reflecting clearly a robust economy in Texas.

Worth mentioning also is that there are another three metropolitan areas in Texas that just missed 1 million jobs mark which we use as a cutoff point to form the top-35 list of metropolitan areas in this chapter. These three areas are Fort Worth-Arlington, San Antonio-New Braunfels, and Austin-Round Rock, together counting nearly 3 million jobs.

Number 11 to 20 Metropolitan Areas

11. Seattle-Bellevue-Everett, WA: 1.6 million jobs ($49,200)

12. Anaheim-Santa Ana-Irvine, CA: 1.6 million jobs ($39,990)

13. Denver-Aurora-Lakewood, CO: 1.4 million jobs ($42,140)

14. San Diego-Carlsbad, CA: 1.4 million jobs ($41,190)

15. Riverside-San Bernardino-Ontario, CA: 1.4 million jobs ($35,450)

16. St. Louis, MO-IL: 1.3 million jobs ($37,090)

17. Baltimore-Columbia-Towson, MD: 1.3 million jobs ($42,560)

18. Nassau County-Suffolk County, NY: 1.3 million jobs ($42,240)

19. Tampa-St. Petersburg-Clearwater, FL: 1.3 million jobs ($34,070)

20. Warren-Troy-Farmington Hills, MI: 1.2 million jobs ($37,980)

Together, the 10 metropolitan areas ranked between #11 and #20 provide nearly 14 million jobs across 7 states. Among them, 3 metropolitan areas are in California, including Anaheim-Santa Ana-Irvine, San Diego-Carlsbad and Riverside-San Bernardino-Ontario, with 4.3 million jobs. In California, the largest metropolitan area is Los Angeles-Long Beach-Glendale, ranked #2 above with 4.2 million jobs.

The Seattle-Bellevue-Everett area in the State of Washington offers 1.6 million jobs with a median salary of $49,200, the highest in this group ranked #11 to #20.

Considering that the State of Washington does not levy a state income tax, a salary of $49,200 in Washington is more valuable than the same salary in states that impose such tax.

Number 21 to 35 Metropolitan Areas

21. Orlando-Kissimmee-Sanford, FL: 1.2 million jobs ($31,410)

22. Charlotte-Concord-Gastonia, NC-SC: 1.2 million jobs ($36,970)

23. Newark, NJ-PA: 1.2 million jobs ($45,140)

24. Pittsburgh, PA: 1.1 million jobs ($36,870)

25. Portland-Vancouver-Hillsboro, OR-WA: 1.1 million jobs ($41,370)

26. Miami-Miami Beach-Kendall, FL: 1.1 million jobs ($33,120)

27. Oakland-Hayward-Berkeley, CA: 1.1 million jobs ($47,520)

28. San Francisco-Redwood City-South San Francisco, CA: 1.1 million jobs ($57,300)

29. San Jose-Sunnyvale-Santa Clara, CA: 1.0 million jobs ($59,700)

30. Kansas City, MO-KS: 1.0 million jobs ($37,830)

31. Cincinnati, OH-KY-IN: 1.0 million jobs ($37,200)

32. Cleveland-Elyria, OH: 1.0 million jobs ($37,830)

33. Columbus, OH: 1.0 million jobs ($37,490)

34. Montgomery County-Bucks County-Chester County, PA: 1.0 million jobs ($40,640)

35. Indianapolis-Carmel-Anderson, IN: 1.0 million jobs ($36,030)

The remaining 15 metropolitan areas that each provides at least 1 million jobs are spread across 13 states. Together, these 15 areas offer over 16 million jobs.

Among these metropolitan areas, the San Jose-Sunnyvale-Santa Clara area boasts the highest median wage of $59,700. Silicon Valley, the leading high technology region in the world, is located in Santa Clara County.

Ten Highest Paying Metropolitan Areas

In the above, the metropolitan areas are ranked by the number of the jobs they offer. Below we present the top 10 metropolitan areas, ranked now by their median salary, from high to low:

1. San Jose-Sunnyvale-Santa Clara, CA: 1.0 million jobs ($59,700)

2. San Francisco-Redwood City-South San Francisco,

CA: 1.1 million jobs ($57,300)

3. California-Lexington Park, MD: 0.0 million jobs ($56,040)

4. Washington-Arlington-Alexandria, DC-VA-MD-WV: 2.5 million jobs ($53,140)

5. Boston-Cambridge-Newton, MA NECTA Division: 1.8 million jobs ($52,770)

6. Framingham, MA NECTA Division: 0.2 million jobs ($50,910)

7. Trenton, NJ: 0.2 million jobs ($50,730)

8. Seattle-Bellevue-Everett, WA: 1.6 million jobs ($49,200)

9. Silver Spring-Frederick-Rockville, MD: 0.6 million jobs ($49,180)

10. San Rafael, CA: 0.1 million jobs ($48,550).

These top ranked metropolitan areas, in terms of salary, together provide 9 million jobs. The San Jose-Sunnyvale-Santa Clara area has a concentration of world renown, leading technology companies and has the highest median salary among all metropolitan areas in the U.S.

In total, 3 of the top 10 areas are in California, 3 in Maryland, 2 in Massachusetts, 1 in New Jersey and 1 in

Washington State.

***

This chapter explained some of the ways in which geographical distribution of occupations differs from state to state, and from one metropolitan area to another, while the previous chapter examined the massive differences in occupations that are attributed to education requirements.

Other than job duties, geographic location and education requirements are likely the two most important factors that explain the significant differences that occupations have in wages, unemployment rate, and employment outlook.

5 HIGHEST PAYING JOBS

There is no way I can justify my salary level, but I'm learning to live with it.

— *Drew Carey*

We can assure ourselves that when the American actor and comedian Drew Carey was quoted saying the above, he was not complaining about an unsatisfactory salary he earned. Quite on the contrary, he probably was making a reference to an extraordinary salary he was taking home, half proudly and half showing off.

Of course, when people achieve stardom, along with popularity and fame, they attract a great deal of money, too. Apart from motion picture stars, TV celebrities, and Olympic champions, many regular wage earners take home generous salaries that will be really eye opening to many of us.

Previously in this book, we took a look at what major groups of occupations are available in the U.S. We saw the huge differences in term of the median wage not only between these major groups but also within any major group of jobs.

In this chapter, let us look beyond the major groups and dive deeper into the detailed occupation level. We will find out, among all detailed occupations across all major groups, which detailed jobs are highest paying.

As mentioned previously, there are 820 detailed occupations. Obviously, the limited space provided within this little book does not allow us to fully list out all the 820 occupations.

Instead, in this chapter, we will compare and contrast the best very paying occupation and the worst, and show how different they are.

We then move on to present the top 100 highest paying occupations, ranked according to their median salaries.

But before we discuss these occupations, we will introduce a second statistical term used in this book, the 90th percentile wage. Recall that we have introduced the median wage before in this book.

What Is the 90th Percentile Wage

So far till this point in the book, we have used the median

wage as a yardstick to compare how well an occupation pays the worker.

Anticipating that the majority of the readership might not be familiar with the concept of the median wage, we note here once again that the median wage is the *wage received by an average person* in an occupation, at the risk of excessive repetition.

Another way of intuiting about the median wage is that the median wage is the *typical wage* paid in an occupation.

In addition to the median, here we introduce another statistical concept of the 90th percentile wage. The 90th percentile wage is the wage that is better than 90% of the salaries paid to workers in an occupation. Thus, it measures how well we can do beyond being an average worker.

It might not be realistic to expect ourselves to be **the very top** performer, but it is entirely achievable to work hard enough and smart enough to get ahead of 90% of our colleagues.

If we are paid better than 90% of the people out there, we are by definition **rich** because rich or not is a relative concept by comparison with our fellow citizens. If we take home a wage more than 90% of what other people are paid, we are rich.

Therefore, in this book, we measure the wage paid to an average person using the median wage, and we measure how rich a job can make us using the 90th percentile wage.

One more note. Even though the Department of Labor data is comprehensive, the 90th percentile wage is not available for a small number of detailed occupations. In those case, estimates of the 90th percentile wages are formed in this book using other data available in the database, using a proprietary method developed by the author of this book.

Okay, if you are scratching your head and are getting intimidated by the jargons in statistics, be assured that no more statistics junky terms will be introduced in the book beyond these two. Relax and enjoy the rest of the book!

Best and Worst Paying Occupations

As demonstrated already in this book, jobs are not created equal. Just look around at the people we know or interact with in our daily lives. From grocery store clerks, to gas station employees, to restaurant waitresses, to construction workers, to computer programmers, to policemen in uniforms, to banker wearing suits and ties, to consultants hauling suitcases, to corporate executives talking in the news, to small business owners, or to freelancer writers, it is not hard to tell that they lead very different lives, with a wide range of tradeoffs between work and personal life, between stress and easy hours, and between effort and reward.

Some jobs are constantly in high demand and enjoy a

tremendous level of job security, while other jobs are very competitive and are crowded with job applicants with indiscernible skill sets.

Some jobs are new creations of this digital age and show a strong future, while other jobs in the sunset industry sectors are endangered and are disappearing, fast.

Some jobs are paying a considerably larger sum of money than other jobs, far above the national median wage, while some other jobs are paying far less.

In some occupations, no matter how hard we work on the job, we will ever be able to make as much as in other occupations. No matter how dedicated we are toward the job, it would still be impossible for us to get ahead. It might not sound fair, but it is the way things are. We have to face this fact and deal with it.

How much a job pays is frequently the number one consideration in our mind when we make a profession decision, especially for younger people who place less importance on work life balance. Instead, they want to go out there to work as hard as possible and make as much money as possible.

How far apart can the two ends of the wage spectrum be?

In the employment statistics released by the U.S. Department of Labor in 2017, there are 156 million workers

in 820 occupations in the U.S. The median salary of the 156 million workers is $37,040 per year. However, the median salary varies wildly from one occupation to another.

The lowest median salary is $19,290, paid to game dealers. Yes, game dealers are those ladies and gentlemen working at casinos who stand behind tables operating games of chance by dealing cards or blocks to players, or operate other gaming equipment.

Although game dealers work so closely to money and chips, they make meager salaries. Granted that many game dealers receive a good amount of tips which might not be reported and not accounted for in the government statistics, the tips are not expected to change the picture entirely.

The next lowest is $19,440, paid to food preparation and serving workers, including fast food workers.

These two salaries, paid to average game dealers and food prep and serving workers, are roughly only half of $37,040, the median salary across all occupations.

This means that if we ended up being a game dealer or a food prep worker, even an average guy out there in other occupations would be making money twice as fast as we do. It would not sound that good for us.

Let us now turn toward the high end of the median salary spectrum, and see how it compares with the median salaries of game dealers and food prep workers, both just

slightly more than $19,000.

The highest median salary across all 820 occupations is $247,339 paid to anesthesiologists. That is right, that is indeed roughly a quarter million dollars, and that is what even an average anesthesiologist takes home every year.

Compared to what an average food prep worker makes, this is 13 × $19,000. Do not forget this is what an average anesthesiologist earns; really good ones can make even much more.

Said another way, it takes an average food prep worker 13 years to earn as much as an average anesthesiologist grosses in a single year. Now, how many 13 years do we have in our lifetime? Not many.

Nothing else needs to be said about the stunning disparity here.

The second highest median salary across all occupations is $232,028 paid to surgeons. This is roughly 12 × $19,000. A similar story; it takes a food prep worker 12 years to earn as much as an anesthesiologist makes in a single year. Isn't it astonishing!

Recall that the median salary is the salary paid to an average worker in an occupation. Can the gap between the best paying and worst paying occupations be even wider, if we compare not the average workers but good workers?

The 90th percentile salary is a salary that is better than those of 90% of the workers. So, if we excel in at our job, we expect to be paid higher than the average worker.

But how much higher?

The lowest 90th percentile salary across all occupations is $25,290, paid to fast food cooks, not much higher than their median salary of $19,860.

For anesthesiologists, the 90th percentile salary of anesthesiologists is a magnificent $413,057, the highest 90th percentile salary across all occupations. (Compare it to the median salary of $247,339.)

Comparing anesthesiologists and fast food cooks, their 90th percentile salaries differ by a sensational 16+ times, more than the difference measured by the median salary.

Clearly, measured by salary, the disparity between jobs is enormous. Of course, our goal is to shun low paying jobs but pursue good paying ones. What are the best paying jobs? Read on.

Concentration of Best Paying Jobs

Now let us now find out about the top 100 best paying jobs ranked by the median wage. For each of these top ranked jobs, its 90th percentile salary is also provided for us to see how good its pay can become, when we climb into the group of the top 10% performers of the occupation.

These 100 jobs are quite concentrated, with 90 out of 100 falling into only 6 major occupation groups. Recall there are in total 22 major occupation groups. These 6 major groups are:

- Healthcare practitioners and technical occupations (22 out of 100)

- Management occupations (22 out of 100)

- Architecture and engineering occupations (17 out of 100)

- Life, physical, and social science occupations (11 out of 100)

- Computer and mathematical occupations (10 out of 100)

- Education, training, and library occupations (8 out of 100).

If getting paid a top wage is highly important to you, then going for an occupation in these six major occupational groups is your best bet.

Okay, here are the top 100 best paying jobs, ranked according to the median wage, from the high to low.

Number 1 to 10 Best Paying Jobs

1. Anesthesiologists: $247,339 (median wage), $413,057

(90th percentile wage)

2. Surgeons: $232,028 (median wage), $387,486 (90th percentile wage)

3. Obstetricians and Gynecologists: $214,963 (median wage), $358,989 (90th percentile wage)

4. Oral and Maxillofacial Surgeons: $213,642 (median wage), $356,782 (90th percentile wage)

5. Orthodontists: $209,890 (median wage), $350,516 (90th percentile wage)

6. Physicians and Surgeons, All Other: $206,920 (median wage), $345,556 (90th percentile wage)

7. Internists, General: $196,380 (median wage), $327,955 (90th percentile wage)

8. Psychiatrists: $194,740 (median wage), $325,216 (90th percentile wage)

9. Family and General Practitioners: $190,490 (median wage), $318,118 (90th percentile wage)

10. Chief Executives: $181,210 (median wage), $302,621 (90th percentile wage)

It is well known that doctors make a lot of money, but it is still shocking that medical professions take 8 out of the top 10 spots.

Anesthesiologists make the most, with the average anesthesiologists take home $247,339 every year. Yes, a quarter million dollars! If you are a good anesthesiologist and do better than 90% of the anesthesiologists, you take home $413,057, a glaring 11 times of the national median wage of $37,040.

Only #8, psychiatrists, and #10, chief executives, are not medical professions among the top 10 spots, although we might argue that psychiatrists are also related to human healthcare (mental health). Both take home an awesome salary each year.

Number 11 to 20 Best Paying Jobs

11. Dentists, All Other Specialists: $173,000 (median wage), $288,910 (90th percentile wage)

12. Pediatricians, General: $168,990 (median wage), $282,213 (90th percentile wage)

13. Nurse Anesthetists: $160,270 (median wage), $267,651 (90th percentile wage)

14. Dentists, General: $153,900 (median wage), $257,013 (90th percentile wage)

15. Computer and Information Systems Managers: $135,800 (median wage), $226,786 (90th percentile wage)

16. Architectural and Engineering Managers: $134,730 (median wage), $207,400 (90th percentile wage)

17. Marketing Managers: $131,180 (median wage), $219,071 (90th percentile wage)

18. Petroleum Engineers: $128,230 (median wage), $214,144 (90th percentile wage)

19. Airline Pilots, Copilots, and Flight Engineers: $127,820 (median wage), $213,459 (90th percentile wage)

20. Prosthodontists: $126,050 (median wage), $210,504 (90th percentile wage)

Between #11 and #20, healthcare related jobs still take 5 out of the 10 spots (#11-14 and #20). Nurses generally make far less than doctors, due to a different level of training required and responsibility assumed at the job.

However, it is surprising to see that nurse anesthetists (#13) actually make a lot of money: An average nurse anesthetist earns $160,270, while the good ones take home more than a quarter million dollars at $267,651.

The other 5 spots between #11 and #20 are taken by computer and information systems managers (#15), architectural and engineering managers (#16), marketing managers (#17), petroleum engineers (#18) and airline pilots, copilots, and flight engineers (#19).

These are all professional jobs that require substantial education and training. Except for marketing managers, the other four are all engineering or technology jobs.

Number 21 to 30 Best Paying Jobs

21. Judges, Magistrate Judges, and Magistrates: $125,880 (median wage), $183,570 (90th percentile wage)

22. Podiatrists: $124,830 (median wage), $208,466 (90th percentile wage)

23. Air Traffic Controllers: $122,410 (median wage), $172,680 (90th percentile wage)

24. Pharmacists: $122,230 (median wage), $157,950 (90th percentile wage)

25. Financial Managers: $121,750 (median wage), $203,323 (90th percentile wage)

26. Natural Sciences Managers: $119,850 (median wage), $200,150 (90th percentile wage)

27. Lawyers: $118,160 (median wage), $197,327 (90th percentile wage)

28. Sales Managers: $117,960 (median wage), $196,993 (90th percentile wage)

29. Compensation and Benefits Managers: $116,240 (median wage), $199,950 (90th percentile wage)

30. Physicists: $115,870 (median wage), $189,560 (90th percentile wage)

Between #21 to #30, only two are healthcare related jobs (#22 and #24), while non-healthcare related occupations show up more, including judges (#21), air traffic controllers (#23), financial managers (#25), science jobs (#26 and #30), lawyers (#27), sales managers (#28), and compensation and benefits managers (#29).

It is a little surprising that lawyers, while making decent earnings, are ranked only #27, somewhat lower than expected. Maybe the field has become overcrowded with many graduating from law schools each year.

Number 31 to 40 Best Paying Jobs

31. Computer Hardware Engineers: $115,080 (median wage), $172,010 (90th percentile wage)

32. Political Scientists: $114,290 (median wage), $160,290 (90th percentile wage)

33. Computer and Information Research Scientists: $111,840 (median wage), $169,680 (90th percentile wage)

34. Purchasing Managers: $111,590 (median wage), $177,560 (90th percentile wage)

35. Law Teachers, Postsecondary: $111,210 (median

wage), $185,721 (90th percentile wage)

36. Aerospace Engineers: $109,650 (median wage), $160,290 (90th percentile wage)

37. Public Relations and Fundraising Managers: $107,320 (median wage), $205,110 (90th percentile wage)

38. Human Resources Managers: $106,910 (median wage), $193,550 (90th percentile wage)

39. Software Developers, Systems Software: $106,860 (median wage), $163,220 (90th percentile wage)

40. Optometrists: $106,140 (median wage), $192,050 (90th percentile wage)

Here software developers show up for the first time, ranked at #39. Two other jobs are also computer related (#31 and #33), and one is an engineering job (#36).

The rest in this tier are a diversified mix of political scientists, law teacher, purchasing managers, public relation managers, human resource managers, and optometrists.

Number 41 to 50 Best Paying Jobs

41. Training and Development Managers: $105,830 (median wage), $184,990 (90th percentile wage)

42. Mathematicians: $105,810 (median wage), $160,310 (90th percentile wage)

43. Managers, All Other: $104,970 (median wage), $172,570 (90th percentile wage)

44. Astronomers: $104,740 (median wage), $165,140 (90th percentile wage)

45. Nuclear Engineers: $102,220 (median wage), $152,420 (90th percentile wage)

46. Physician Assistants: $101,480 (median wage), $142,210 (90th percentile wage)

47. Computer Network Architects: $101,210 (median wage), $158,590 (90th percentile wage)

48. Economists: $101,050 (median wage), $181,060 (90th percentile wage)

49. Nurse Practitioners: $100,910 (median wage), $140,930 (90th percentile wage)

50. Advertising and Promotions Managers: $100,810 (median wage), $168,353 (90th percentile wage)

The occupations in the tier of #41 to #50 are quite diversified. Interesting to note among them are mathematicians (#42). A lot of people think of mathematicians as geeky; however, people might not know that mathematicians are not only smart but also paid well.

The #44 spot is astronomers. There are only a handful astronomers ($44), but compared with their rarity, they appear to make decent but not exceptional salaries.

Number 51 to 60 Best Paying Jobs

51. Actuaries: $100,610 (median wage), $186,250 (90th percentile wage)

52. Software Developers, Applications: $100,080 (median wage), $157,590 (90th percentile wage)

53. Sales Engineers: $100,000 (median wage), $166,500 (90th percentile wage)

54. Nurse Midwives: $99,770 (median wage), $142,510 (90th percentile wage)

55. Materials Scientists: $99,430 (median wage), $157,750 (90th percentile wage)

56. Health Specialties Teachers, Postsecondary: $99,360 (median wage), $165,931 (90th percentile wage)

57. General and Operations Managers: $99,310 (median wage), $165,848 (90th percentile wage)

58. Electronics Engineers, Except Computer: $99,210 (median wage), $155,330 (90th percentile wage)

59. Chemical Engineers: $98,340 (median wage), $158,800 (90th percentile wage)

60. Engineering Teachers, Postsecondary: $97,530 (median wage), $176,560 (90th percentile wage)

The occupations in the tier of #51 to #60 are also a good mix of different lines of work. Three are in science and engineering (#55, #58, and #59), and two are postsecondary teaching jobs ($56 and #60).

The best paying occupation in this tier is actuaries (#1), with the average worker paid a median salary of $100,610 and good workers paid a 90th percentile salary of $186,250.

Actuaries are really just mathematicians or statisticians specialized in the insurance industry. They analyze the financial costs of risk and uncertainty.

Actuaries use mathematics, statistics, and financial theory to assess the risk of potential events, helping businesses and clients develop policies that minimize the cost of that risk.

Number 61 to 70 Best Paying Jobs

61. Engineers, All Other: $97,300 (median wage), $152,970 (90th percentile wage)

62. Industrial Production Managers: $97,140 (median wage), $165,450 (90th percentile wage)

63. Medical and Health Services Managers: $96,540 (median wage), $172,240 (90th percentile wage)

64. Physical Scientists, All Other: $96,070 (median wage), $155,000 (90th percentile wage)

65. Economics Teachers, Postsecondary: $95,770 (median wage), $195,730 (90th percentile wage)

66. Psychologists, All Other: $95,710 (median wage), $127,710 (90th percentile wage)

67. Electrical Engineers: $94,210 (median wage), $149,040 (90th percentile wage)

68. Mining and Geological Engineers, Including Mining Safety Engineers: $93,720 (median wage), $160,510 (90th percentile wage)

69. Marine Engineers and Naval Architects: $93,350 (median wage), $152,450 (90th percentile wage)

70. Materials Engineers: $93,310 (median wage), $148,840 (90th percentile wage)

The occupations in the tier of #61 to #70 are dominated by science and engineering occupations, including #61, #64, #67 to #70).

There are also two healthcare occupations (#63 and #66) and one postsecondary teaching job (#65).

Notice that in the tier, none of the occupations pay 6-figure median salaries, but they are close to 6-figures.

Number 71 to 80 Best Paying Jobs

71. Information Security Analysts: $92,600 (median wage), $147,290 (90th percentile wage)

72. Education Administrators, Elementary and Secondary School: $92,510 (median wage), $135,770 (90th percentile wage)

73. Atmospheric and Space Scientists: $92,460 (median wage), $140,830 (90th percentile wage)

74. Administrative Law Judges, Adjudicators, and Hearing Officers: $92,110 (median wage), $162,400 (90th percentile wage)

75. Agricultural Sciences Teachers, Postsecondary: $91,580 (median wage), $153,250 (90th percentile wage)

76. Nuclear Power Reactor Operators: $91,170 (median wage), $121,570 (90th percentile wage)

77. Education Administrators, Postsecondary: $90,760 (median wage), $179,250 (90th percentile wage)

78. Personal Financial Advisors: $90,530 (median wage), $151,185 (90th percentile wage)

79. Administrative Services Managers: $90,050 (median wage), $159,330 (90th percentile wage)

80. Art Directors: $89,820 (median wage), $166,400 (90th percentile wage)

The occupations in the tier of #71 to #80 are highly diversified, including three education related jobs (#72, #75, and #77).

The best median salary within this tier is paid to information security analysts (#71). Information security analysts plan and carry out security measures to protect an organization's computer networks and systems.

Their responsibilities are continually expanding as cyberattacks gain sophistication and cause large financial and reputational losses.

Most information security analysts work for computer companies, consulting firms, or business and financial companies.

The last spot in this tier is taken by art directors. Art directors are responsible for the visual style and images in magazines, newspapers, product packaging, and movie and television productions. They create the overall design of a project and direct others who develop artwork and layouts.

About 3 in 5 art directors were self-employed in 2016. Others worked for advertising and public relations firms, newspaper and magazine publishers, motion picture and video industries, and specialized design services firms.

Number 81 to 90 Best Paying Jobs

81. Geoscientists, Except Hydrologists and Geographers: $89,780 (median wage), $189,020 (90th percentile wage)

82. Construction Managers: $89,300 (median wage), $158,330 (90th percentile wage)

83. Transportation, Storage, and Distribution Managers: $89,190 (median wage), $152,730 (90th percentile wage)

84. Veterinarians: $88,770 (median wage), $161,070 (90th percentile wage)

85. Computer Systems Analysts: $87,220 (median wage), $137,690 (90th percentile wage)

86. Health and Safety Engineers, Except Mining Safety Engineers and Inspectors: $86,720 (median wage), $134,110 (90th percentile wage)

87. Computer Occupations, All Other: $86,510 (median wage), $133,890 (90th percentile wage)

88. Forestry and Conservation Science Teachers, Postsecondary: $85,880 (median wage), $144,820 (90th percentile wage)

89. Biomedical Engineers: $85,620 (median wage), $134,620 (90th percentile wage)

90. Atmospheric, Earth, Marine, and Space Sciences Teachers, Postsecondary: $85,410 (median wage), $161,220 (90th percentile wage)

The occupations in the tier of #81 to #90 are dominated by science and engineering occupations (#81, #86, and #88 to #90). There are also two computer related occupations (#85 and #87).

Geoscientists (#81) the best paying occupation in this tier, with an attractive median salary of $89,780 and a magnificent 90th percentile salary of $189,020.

Geoscientists study the physical aspects of the Earth, such as its composition, structure, and processes, to learn about its past, present, and future.

Most geoscientists split their time between working indoors in offices and laboratories, and working outdoors.

Doing research and investigations outdoors is commonly called fieldwork and can require irregular working hours and extensive travel to remote locations.

If nature and outdoor activities are your calling, geoscientist jobs are a great fit.

Number 91 to 100 Best Paying Jobs

91. Physical Therapists: $85,400 (median wage), $122,130 (90th percentile wage)

92. Database Administrators: $84,950 (median wage), $129,930 (90th percentile wage)

93. Environmental Engineers: $84,890 (median wage), $130,120 (90th percentile wage)

94. First-Line Supervisors of Police and Detectives: $84,840 (median wage), $134,810 (90th percentile wage)

95. Physics Teachers, Postsecondary: $84,570 (median wage), $164,130 (90th percentile wage)

96. Industrial Engineers: $84,310 (median wage), $129,390 (90th percentile wage)

97. Mechanical Engineers: $84,190 (median wage), $131,350 (90th percentile wage)

98. Civil Engineers: $83,540 (median wage), $132,880 (90th percentile wage)

99. Industrial-Organizational Psychologists: $82,760 (median wage), $184,380 (90th percentile wage)

100. Biochemists and Biophysicists: $82,180 (median wage), $158,410 (90th percentile wage)

The occupations in the tier of #91 to #100 are also dominated by science and engineering occupations (#93, #95 to #98, and #100).

Among the top spots of #51 to #100 of the best paying occupations, slightly more than half are split between engineering jobs (13 out of 50), computer and math related jobs (6 out of 50) and science jobs (7 out of 50) for a total of 26 spots.

There are also 8 management jobs and 7 education, training and library jobs, with the rest 100 spread over other 7 major occupation groups.

So, these are the top 100 jobs in terms of wage, with #100 still making $82,180, more than twice of the all-occupation median wage of $37,040.

After examining these 100 jobs, healthcare practitioners overall stand out as the highest paid professionals, including for example anesthesiologists, surgeons, obstetricians, gynecologists, orthodontists, general internists, psychiatrists, family practitioners, dentists and pediatricians.

Loosely, the next group of best paying occupations include highly specialized professions such as judges, lawyers, petroleum engineers, pilots, marketing managers, and other managerial positions.

Scientists, mathematicians, software developers, computer hardware engineers, computer network architects, actuaries, and other engineers make up the next tier of jobs with decent wages.

Other than decent wages, all these top paying jobs share another commonality; that is, they all require higher education and/or years of training.

Indeed, there is no free lunch in this world.

6 FASTEST GROWING JOBS

*Change is the law of life. And those who look only to
the past or present are certain to miss the future.*

— *John F. Kennedy*

B e aware of changes and follow the trend, especially when we make career choices. Joining a profession is a serious decision which has long term implications. Once we make a decision, it will be difficult and costly to reverse that decision to switch to another line of work.

If we join a fast growing, upcoming occupation, a career that rides the trend will be a much easier one than otherwise. If we are unfortunate and end up in a dying occupation, it is likely that it will become a lifelong struggle for us. And it will only get worse as years pass by. Spending a little time now to learn what is hot and what is fading away will for sure pay off handsomely in the years to come.

Even if we have a job already, it is still imperative that we find out whether our current occupation will hold up well in the future. If the answer is no, we might need to start thinking whether we should make a career change to work in a different field with a brighter outlook.

In this chapter, we examine occupational growth outlook projected for the 10-year period of 2016 to 2026, and present the top 100 fastest growing jobs.

Fastest Growing Occupations

Job growth look is an important measure of job security in the future, telling us how well an occupation would do in future: Will it become more popular and more in demand? Or will it become less in demand? Will the need for workers shrink fast as a result?

The big picture first. The total number of jobs in the U.S. was 156.1 million in 2016, and it is projected to grow 7.4% to 167.6 million by 2026. Overall, the U.S. is not losing jobs but instead growing jobs.

However, the growth is not evenly distributed across occupations. Some are growing much faster than others, while some are growing more slowly. There are even occupations that are projected not to grow at all, or even decline over the coming years.

Our goal here in this chapter is to identify the fastest

growing jobs.

According to the data released by the U.S. Department of Labor in October 2017, the most job growth is forecasted to occur to personal care aides, projected to add 754,000 jobs between 2016 and 2026, a 37.4% growth.

Food preparation and serving workers are at the second position with 579,900 jobs to add, a 16.8% growth, while registered nurses will add 437,000, over the same 2016-2026 period, a 14.8% increase.

If we are in these professions, we know we are not going to worry about landing a job or losing a job. We can rest assured that our jobs are secure.

The above occupations are the top three occupations that are projected to grow the most by the absolute number.

By percentage growth, here are the top 10 jobs, projected over the 10-year period of 2016 – 2026. The median wages of these occupations are also provided alongside the percentage growth.

1. Solar photovoltaic installers: 105.3% (job growth), $39,240 (median wage)

2. Wind turbine service technicians: 96.1% (job growth), $52,260 (median wage)

3. Personal care aides: 37.4% (job growth), $21,920

(median wage)

4. Physician assistants: 37.4% (job growth), $101,480 (median wage)

5. Nurse practitioners: 36% (job growth), $100,910 (median wage)

6. Statisticians: 33.4% (job growth), $80,500 (median wage)

7. Physical therapist assistants: 30.8% (job growth), $56,610 (median wage)

8. Software developers, applications: 30.5% (job growth), $100,080 (median wage)

9. Bicycle repairers: 29.4% (job growth), $27,630 (median wage)

10. Mathematicians: 29.4% (job growth), $105,810 (median wage)

All of the top 10 fastest growing jobs are projected to expand much much faster than the average growth of 7.4%.

The largest growth of 105.3% for solar photovoltaic installer jobs is more than 14 times of 7.4%. Even the last spot on the top-10 list, a 29.4% growth for mathematicians, is still 4 times of the average 7.4% growth.

Demand for solar photovoltaic installers and wind

turbine service technicians will grow 105.3% and 96.1%, respectively, between 2016 and 2026, taking the top two percentage grow spots among all occupations.

Both promising alternative energy sources to fossil fuels, solar power panel and wind turbine installation is expected to see a huge expansion. It makes sense that, as a result, technicians to install and service solar photovoltaic panels and wind turbines will be in hot demand.

If you are fond of hands-on field work, this occupation is an excellent choice.

Healthcare occupations are clear winners of the job growth. In this top-10 list, three are healthcare occupations, including physician assistants, nurse practitioners, and physical therapist assistants, growing 37.4%, 36%, and 30.8%, respectively, between 2016 and 2026. Both physician assistants and nurse practitioners typically earn 6-figure salaries.

Statisticians and mathematicians are also projected to grow a 33.4% and 29.4%, respectively, between 2016 and 2026. Statisticians make a typical, handsome salary of $80,500, while mathematicians take home even more at $105,810.

It is, however, interesting to note that not all fast-growing jobs are paying well. For instance, in the above 10 jobs, personal care aides (#3) is paid a meager median annual salary of $21,920, and bicycle repairers (#9) a poor median salary of $27,630.

It is evident that fast growth does not necessarily equate good pay. Despite a fast growth, if a job does not pay well, it is not attractive and is not something we should aim for.

Let us be ambitious and look for attractive jobs that not only pay well but also are project to grow fast at the same time.

Fastest Growing Jobs That Pay Well

So, let us modify our ranking criteria. Recall that the national median wage across all occupations is $37,040, per the latest wage statistics released by the U.S. Department of Labor in 2017.

Let us be ambitious and shoot for jobs that pay at least a median salary of $74,080, twice of the all-occupation median wage of $37,040.

The threshold of $74,080 is purely subjective, but it is a reasonably good pay nonetheless. I would be happy to have a job paying $74,080 whose demand is projected to grow fast.

Among all occupations whose median earning is above $74,080, let us identify the 100 jobs that are projected to grow the fastest over the ten-year period of 2016 – 2026.

It turns out that these 100 jobs are quite concentrated.

Although these 100 jobs fall into 11 major occupation groups, 95 out of 100 belong to only 7 major occupation groups. Recall there are in total 22 major occupational groups.

These 11 major groups are:

- Healthcare Practitioners and Technical Occupations (28 out of 100)

- Education, Training, and Library Occupations (17 out of 100)

- Management Occupations (16 out of 100)

- Computer and Mathematical Occupations (11 out of 100)

- Architecture and Engineering Occupations (10 out of 100)

- Life, Physical, and Social Science Occupations (9 out of 100)

- Business and Financial Operations Occupations (4 out of 100)

- Arts, Design, Entertainment, Sports, and Media Occupations (2 out of 100)

- Construction and Extraction Occupations (1 out of 100)

- Protective Service Occupations (1 out of 100)

- Legal Occupations (1 out of 100)

Clearly, healthcare jobs, education jobs, and computer and math jobs are big winners of the growth outlook.

Now let us take a look at the detailed list of top 100 such jobs, ranked by the projected percentage growth between 2016 and 2026, from high to low.

Number I to 10 Fast Growing Jobs

1. Physician assistants: 37.4% (job growth), $101,480 (median wage)

2. Nurse practitioners: 36% (job growth), $100,910 (median wage)

3. Statisticians: 33.4% (job growth), $80,500 (median wage)

4. Software developers, applications: 30.5% (job growth), $100,080 (median wage)

5. Mathematicians: 29.4% (job growth), $105,810 (median wage)

6. Information security analysts: 28.4% (job growth), $92,600 (median wage)

7. Genetic counselors: 28.3% (job growth), $74,120

(median wage)

8. Operations research analysts: 27.4% (job growth), $79,200 (median wage)

9. Health specialties teachers, postsecondary: 25.9% (job growth), $99,360 (median wage)

10. Physical therapists: 25% (job growth), $85,400 (median wage)

The top 10 fastest growing occupations among all occupations that pay at least a $74,080 median wage are projected to have a growth ranging from 37.4% to 25% from 2016 to 2026.

Among them, it is striking that 5 out 10 are healthcare related: Physician assistants (#1), nurse practitioners (#2), genetic counselors (#7), health specialties teachers (#9), and physical therapists (#10).

Three out of 10 are statistics and math related occupations: Statisticians (#3), mathematicians (#5), and operations research analysts (#8).

Number 11 to 20 Fast Growing Jobs

11. Actuaries: 22.5% (job growth), $100,610 (median wage)

12. Occupational therapists: 21.2% (job growth), $81,910

(median wage)

13. Nurse midwives: 20.6% (job growth), $99,770 (median wage)

14. Audiologists: 20.4% (job growth), $75,980 (median wage)

15. Medical and health services managers: 19.8% (job growth), $96,540 (median wage)

16. Computer and information research scientists: 19.2% (job growth), $111,840 (median wage)

17. Financial managers: 18.7% (job growth), $121,750 (median wage)

18. Business teachers, postsecondary: 18.1% (job growth), $77,490 (median wage)

19. Veterinarians: 18.1% (job growth), $88,770 (median wage)

20. Obstetricians and gynecologists: 17.9% (job growth), $214,963 (median wage)

Number 11 to 20 fastest growing occupations paying at least a $74,080 median wage are projected to have a strong growth ranging from 22.5% to 17.9% from 2016 to 2026.

Among them, obstetricians and gynecologists are best paid at $214,963, followed by financial managers at

$121,750, computer and information research scientists at $111,840, and actuaries at $100,610, all 6-figure earners.

Number 21 to 30 Fast Growing Jobs

21. Anesthesiologists: 17.8% (job growth), $247,339 (median wage)

22. Pediatricians, general: 17.8% (job growth), $168,990 (median wage)

23. Speech-language pathologists: 17.5% (job growth), $74,680 (median wage)

24. Dentists, general: 17.5% (job growth), $153,900 (median wage)

25. Optometrists: 17.3% (job growth), $106,140 (median wage)

26. Orthodontists: 17.3% (job growth), $209,890 (median wage)

27. Oral and maxillofacial surgeons: 17.2% (job growth), $213,642 (median wage)

28. Prosthodontists: 17.2% (job growth), $126,050 (median wage)

29. Internists, general: 16.9% (job growth), $196,380 (median wage)

30. Surgeons: 16.8% (job growth), $232,028 (median wage)

Number 21 to 30 fastest growing occupations paying at least a $74,080 median wage are projected to have a healthy growth ranging from 17.8% to 16.8% till 2026.

Among them, anesthesiologists are best paid at $247,339, the best paying occupation among all occupations with a projected growth of 17.8%, nearly two time and a half of the average growth of 7.4%.

All of the 10 jobs in this tier are healthcare jobs, and all of them are paying 6-figure salaries with a percentage growth of at least 16.8%.

No question that healthcare occupations will hold up very well in the years to come.

Number 31 to 40 Fast Growing Jobs

31. Family and general practitioners: 16.5% (job growth), $190,490 (median wage)

32. Nurse anesthetists: 16% (job growth), $160,270 (median wage)

33. Biological science teachers, postsecondary: 15.1% (job growth), $76,650 (median wage)

34. Engineering teachers, postsecondary: 14.5% (job

growth), $97,530 (median wage)

35. Petroleum engineers: 14.5% (job growth), $128,230 (median wage)

36. Physicists: 14.5% (job growth), $115,870 (median wage)

37. Personal financial advisors: 14.4% (job growth), $90,530 (median wage)

38. Geoscientists, except hydrologists and geographers: 13.9% (job growth), $89,780 (median wage)

39. Physicians and surgeons, all other: 13.3% (job growth), $206,920 (median wage)

40. Medical scientists, except epidemiologists: 13.2% (job growth), $80,530 (median wage)

Number 31 to 40 fastest growing occupations paying at least a $74,080 median wage are projected to have a healthy growth ranging from 16.5% to 13.2% between 2016 to 2026.

Among them, physicians and surgeons are paid a marvelous median salary of $206,920, followed by family and general practitioners at $190,490, nurse anesthetists at $160,270, petroleum engineers at $128,230, and physicists at $115,870.

Two of the 10 occupations in this tier are postsecondary teachers: Biological science teachers and engineering teachers, both paid well and enjoying robust job growth outlook.

Number 41 to 50 Fast Growing Jobs

41. Psychiatrists: 13.1% (job growth), $194,740 (median wage)

42. Law teachers, postsecondary: 12.2% (job growth), $111,210 (median wage)

43. Elevator installers and repairers: 12.1% (job growth), $78,890 (median wage)

44. Management analysts: 12% (job growth), $81,330 (median wage)

45. Dentists, all other specialists: 12% (job growth), $173,000 (median wage)

46. Atmospheric and space scientists: 12% (job growth), $92,460 (median wage)

47. Computer and information systems managers: 11.9% (job growth), $135,800 (median wage)

48. Radiation therapists: 11.9% (job growth), $80,160 (median wage)

49. Database administrators: 11.5% (job growth), $84,950 (median wage)

50. Marine engineers and naval architects: 11.5% (job growth), $93,350 (median wage)

Number 41 to 50 fastest growing occupations paying at least a $74,080 median wage are projected to have a healthy growth ranging from 13.1% to 11.5% till 2026.

Among them, psychiatrists make the best earning at $194,790, followed by dentists at $173,000, computer and information systems managers at $135,800, and law teachers at $111,210.

Number 51 to 60 Fast Growing Jobs

51. Construction managers: 11.4% (job growth), $89,300 (median wage)

52. Health diagnosing and treating practitioners, all other: 11.4% (job growth), $74,530 (median wage)

53. Biochemists and biophysicists: 11.3% (job growth), $82,180 (median wage)

54. Financial analysts: 10.8% (job growth), $81,760 (median wage)

55. Software developers, systems software: 10.8% (job growth), $106,860 (median wage)

56. Civil engineers: 10.6% (job growth), $83,540 (median wage)

57. Economics teachers, postsecondary: 10.6% (job growth), $95,770 (median wage)

58. Architecture teachers, postsecondary: 10.6% (job growth), $79,250 (median wage)

59. Political science teachers, postsecondary: 10.5% (job growth), $79,210 (median wage)

60. Public relations and fundraising managers: 10.4% (job growth), $107,320 (median wage)

Number 51 to 60 fastest growing occupations paying at least a $74,080 median wage are projected to have a healthy growth ranging from 11.4% to 10.4% till 2026.

Among them, Public relations and fundraising managers make the best earning at $107,320, followed by system software developers at $106,860.

Three of the 10 occupations in this tier are postsecondary teachers: Economics teachers, architecture teachers, and political science teachers, all paid well and expecting solid growth.

Number 61 to 70 Fast Growing Jobs

61. Education administrators, all other: 10.4% (job growth), $78,210 (median wage)

62. Training and development managers: 10.3% (job

growth), $105,830 (median wage)

63. Administrative services managers: 10.1% (job growth), $90,050 (median wage)

64. Education administrators, postsecondary: 10% (job growth), $90,760 (median wage)

65. Marketing managers: 10% (job growth), $131,180 (median wage)

66. Astronomers: 10% (job growth), $104,740 (median wage)

67. Physics teachers, postsecondary: 10% (job growth), $84,570 (median wage)

68. Anthropology and archeology teachers, postsecondary: 10% (job growth), $81,350 (median wage)

69. Natural sciences managers: 9.9% (job growth), $119,850 (median wage)

70. Chemistry teachers, postsecondary: 9.9% (job growth), $76,750 (median wage)

Number 61 to 70 fastest growing occupations paying at least a $74,080 median wage are projected to have a healthy growth ranging from 10.4% to 9.9% till 2026.

Among them, 6-figure earners are marketing managers

paid at $131,180, natural sciences managers at $119,850, training and development managers at $105,830, and astronomers at $104,740.

It is interesting that astronomers make just a little over $100,000, lower than many other occupations. But I guess the fun and thrill of the job pays much more than the salary does.

Three of the 10 occupations in this tier are postsecondary teachers: Physics teachers, anthropology and archeology teachers, and chemistry teachers, all paid well and expecting solid growth. In addition, postsecondary education administrators are also on the list here, enjoying good pays and promising outlook.

Number 71 to 80 Fast Growing Jobs

71. Hydrologists: 9.9% (job growth), $80,480 (median wage)

72. Financial examiners: 9.8% (job growth), $79,280 (median wage)

73. Nuclear medicine technologists: 9.8% (job growth), $74,350 (median wage)

74. Industrial engineers: 9.7% (job growth), $84,310 (median wage)

75. Podiatrists: 9.7% (job growth), $124,830 (median

wage)

76. Environmental science teachers, postsecondary: 9.6% (job growth), $78,340 (median wage)

77. Atmospheric, earth, marine, and space sciences teachers, postsecondary: 9.5% (job growth), $85,410 (median wage)

78. Lawyers: 9.4% (job growth), $118,160 (median wage)

79. General and operations managers: 9.1% (job growth), $99,310 (median wage)

80. Psychologists, all other: 9.1% (job growth), $95,710 (median wage)

Number 71 to 80 fastest growing occupations paying at least a $74,080 median wage are projected to have a healthy growth ranging from 9.9% to 9.1% till 2026.

Among them, podiatrists and lawyers are the only two occupations paying typical 6-figure median salaries. General and operations managers and psychologists make very close to 6-figures.

Number 81 to 90 Fast Growing Jobs

81. Computer occupations, all other: 9% (job growth), $86,510 (median wage)

82. Human resources managers: 8.9% (job growth),

$106,910 (median wage)

83. Computer systems analysts: 8.8% (job growth), $87,220 (median wage)

84. Mechanical engineers: 8.8% (job growth), $84,190 (median wage)

85. Electrical engineers: 8.6% (job growth), $94,210 (median wage)

86. Health and safety engineers, except mining safety engineers and inspectors: 8.6% (job growth), $86,720 (median wage)

87. Geography teachers, postsecondary: 8.4% (job growth), $76,810 (median wage)

88. Environmental engineers: 8.3% (job growth), $84,890 (median wage)

89. Computer science teachers, postsecondary: 8% (job growth), $77,570 (median wage)

90. Biological scientists, all other: 7.9% (job growth), $74,790 (median wage)

Number 81 to 90 fastest growing occupations paying at least a $74,080 median wage are projected to have a healthy growth ranging from 9% to 7.9% till 2026.

Human resources managers are the only occupation

paying a 6-figure median salary within this tier, with average electrical engineers paid very close to a 6-figure salary.

Number 91 to 100 Fast Growing Jobs

91. Media and communication equipment workers, all other: 7.9% (job growth), $75,700 (median wage)

92. Education administrators, elementary and secondary school: 7.8% (job growth), $92,510 (median wage)

93. Forestry and conservation science teachers, postsecondary: 7.7% (job growth), $85,880 (median wage)

94. Managers, all other: 7.6% (job growth), $104,970 (median wage)

95. Chemical engineers: 7.6% (job growth), $98,340 (median wage)

96. Agricultural sciences teachers, postsecondary: 7.5% (job growth), $91,580 (median wage)

97. Sales managers: 7.4% (job growth), $117,960 (median wage)

98. Art directors: 7.4% (job growth), $89,820 (median wage)

99. First-line supervisors of firefighting and prevention

workers: 7.2% (job growth), $74,540 (median wage)

100. Biomedical engineers: 7.2% (job growth), $85,620 (median wage)

Number 91 to 100 fastest growing occupations paying at least a $74,080 median wage are projected to have a healthy growth ranging from 7.9% to 7.2% till 2026.

Art directors (#98 above) enjoy a projected job growth of 7.4% which is the average growth across all occupations.

Therefore, #1 to #98 on the top 100 fastest growing occupations that pay at least $74,080 annually are forecasted to grow at or more than the all-occupation average growth of 7.4%.

The remaining 2 occupations on our top-100 list (#99 to #100) are projected to actually grow fewer jobs between 2016 and 2026 than the average.

In this tier of #91 to #100, sales managers make the best median salary of $117,960

If you think the threshold of $74,080 is a good choice, then join an occupation out of the 100 above to ensure that in the future it is going to grow but not remain flat or even shrink.

7 ENDANGERED JOBS

It does not do to leave a live dragon out of your calculations, if you live near him.

— *J.R.R. Tolkien, The Hobbit*

Now that we know which jobs will grow fast in the years to come, let us also learn where the landmines are on the road to landing a great job, and keep their locations in our calculations.

These landmines are the endangered jobs that are expected to disappear over time. Without saying, we are not going to endeavor only to join a vanishing line of work, but to avoid signing up to such an occupation without knowing its future.

In the previous chapter, we touched upon the big picture of job growth in the U.S. between 2016 and 2026, and provided details of the top 100 fastest growing occupations.

According to the occupational outlook published by the U.S. Department of Labor, the total number of jobs in the U.S. was 156.1 million in 2016, and it is projected to grow 7.4% to 167.6 million by 2026.

However, the growth is not evenly distributed across occupations. Some occupations, instead of growing, will even lose jobs over years.

There is sunrise, and there is sunset. Same goes for occupations. We do not need a crystal ball to know that in the not-too-distant future, advances in technology and changing consumer preferences will crush the careers of some people who are very happily employed at this very moment.

Take the case, for example, of the Rust Belt, the region of the United States from the Great Lakes to the Northern Midwest States.

This region used to be called the Manufacturing Belt, Factory Belt, or Steel Belt, and was previously known as the industrial heartland of America.

There is Boom, and there is Bust, and hence its current name: Rust Belt.

Rust refers to the deindustrialization. Since the mid-20th century, the region has been seeing industry declining, due to a variety of economic factors, such as the transfer of manufacturing further West, increased automation, and the decline of the US steel and coal industries.

This fundamental shifting of the economic landscape caused too many job losses, population loss, and urban decay due to the shrinking of its once-powerful industrial sector.

Fundamental structural changes in economic sectors have never stopped. Think for example the rise of personal computers, the Internet, e-mail, tablet computers, smart phones, Facebook, Twitter, Uber, driverless cars, artificially intelligence, and robotics. This list of technological advances can go on and on.

On top of the technological advances, there are also powerful changes in demographic trend and consumer preferences.

All these changes are killing occupations such as mail carrier (we communicate through e-mail, smart phones, or social media instead of letters), taxi dispatchers (who needs them now that we have the Uber app on our smart phones), newspaper reporters (they are being replaced by an infinite number of bloggers and freelance writers), printing workers (who buys newspaper and magazines anymore), insurance underwriter (automated underwriting software can do their job tirelessly 24/7), or travel agents (now many of us use the Internet to research vacations and book trips).

It is expected many other occupations will become career roadkills, too, as robotics and artificial intelligence further mature up.

The only mitigation we have is to become aware of this pattern of constant changes and be vigilant in selecting our careers.

In this chapter, let us first find out the big picture: Which major occupation groups are projected to lose jobs fast? It would be wise to avoid these broad areas of occupations given their forecasted gloomy outlook.

We then go through the details of the top 100 fastest declining jobs, per the job growth projection for the 10-year period of 2016 to 2026.

Declining Major Occupation Groups

The top 100 occupations that are projected to lose job at the fastest rates are spread across 16 major occupation groups. However, 89 of them are concentrated in the following 7 major groups.

- Production Occupations (52 out of 100)

- Office and Administrative Support Occupations (17 out of 100)

- Installation, Maintenance, and Repair Occupations (6 out of 100)

- Business and Financial Operations Occupations (4

out of 100)

- Arts, Design, Entertainment, Sports, and Media Occupations (4 out of 100)

- Protective Service Occupations (3 out of 100)

- Farming, Fishing, and Forestry Occupations (3 out of 100)

Among these 7 major occupation groups, the production occupations group takes 52 out of the top 100 fastest dying occupations. That is more than half of the top 100 spots.

Manufacturing jobs are a major part of production occupations.

Why am I not surprised? Of course not, with American manufacturing jobs been packed up and shipped offshores for the past two decades, it surprises no one that production occupations are endangered and make up more than half of the top 100 fastest vanishing jobs in the U.S.

Unless the trend of outsourcing manufacturing jobs sees a clear reversal, it is wise not to join these occupations at risk.

Office and administrative support occupations are the second largest major occupation group among the top 100 fastest disappearing jobs, taking 17 spots.

With the advancement of personal computers, printers,

the Internet, e-mail, office software such as Microsoft Word, Excel, Outlook, among others, office and admin support work has been largely automated and can be done by regular employees, reducing the demand for dedicated office and admin personnel.

Hence, we'd better not to aspire to join an office and administrate support occupation, but leave those jobs to office automation and maybe artificial intelligence and robot secretaries.

Now, let us take a look at the top 100 fastest disappearing detailed occupations in the U.S. between 2016 and 2026 below.

Number 1 to 10 Fastest Vanishing Jobs

1. Locomotive firers: -78.6% (job decline), $58,230 (median wage)

2. Respiratory therapy technicians: -56.3% (job decline), $49,780 (median wage)

3. Parking enforcement workers: -35.3% (job decline), $37,950 (median wage)

4. Word processors and typists: -33.4% (job decline), $38,740 (median wage)

5. Watch repairers: -28.7% (job decline), $36,740 (median wage)

6. Electronic equipment installers and repairers, motor vehicles: -25.2% (job decline), $32,220 (median wage)

7. Foundry mold and coremakers: -24% (job decline), $34,790 (median wage)

8. Pourers and casters, metal: -23.4% (job decline), $36,180 (median wage)

9. Computer operators: -22.9% (job decline), $42,270 (median wage)

10. Telephone operators: -22.6% (job decline), $37,000 (median wage)

These top 10 fastest disappearing jobs are projected to decline anywhere from 78.6% and 22.6% between 2016 and 2026.

Most of these declining jobs are really old-time jobs. For example, locomotive firers, telephone operators, watch repairers all sound grandpa and grandma jobs. Not surprised at all that these are disappearing fast in the information age of the 21st century.

All occupations in this tier are actually paying decently around or well above the all-occupation median salary of $37,040.

Two jobs, locomotive firers (#1) and respiratory therapy technicians (#2), among the top ten pay significantly above the all-occupation median wage of $37,040, at $58,230 and $49,780, respectively.

Unfortunately, they are fading away at a startling speed. Locomotive firers will lose 78.6% of the jobs between 2016 and 2026; that is, every 3 out of 4 jobs will go away.

Respiratory therapy technicians will lose 56.3% of the jobs; that is, more than half of the jobs will disappear.

Watch repairers will lose 28.7% of the jobs, perhaps because many people do not feel the need for watches anymore as they can easily tell time from cellphones.

Stay away from these occupations if you can.

Number 11 to 20 Fastest Vanishing Jobs

11. Mine shuttle car operators: -21.9% (job decline), $56,450 (median wage)

12. Electromechanical equipment assemblers: -21.3% (job decline), $33,350 (median wage)

13. Data entry keyers: -21.1% (job decline), $30,100 (median wage)

14. Postmasters and mail superintendents: -20.9% (job decline), $71,670 (median wage)

15. Electrical and electronic equipment assemblers: -20.7% (job decline), $31,310 (median wage)

16. Coil winders, tapers, and finishers: -20.6% (job decline), $33,940 (median wage)

17. Grinding and polishing workers, hand: -20.5% (job decline), $28,720 (median wage)

18. Timing device assemblers and adjusters: -19.9% (job decline), $37,040 (median wage)

19. Switchboard operators, including answering service: -19.9% (job decline), $28,030 (median wage)

20. Drilling and boring machine tool setters, operators, and tenders, metal and plastic: -19.4% (job decline), $36,410 (median wage)

These 10 fast disappearing jobs are projected to decline anywhere from 21.9% and 19.4% between 2016 and 2026.

Postal service workers (#14) are paid well, but unfortunately their jobs are having a huge decline, perhaps primarily due to the prevalence of e-mail and marketing directly to our computers and smart phones.

Many occupations in this tier are manufacturing related, for example, a variety of machine operators and equipment assemblers, as the manufacturing jobs have been outsourced to countries where labor costs are significantly lower than the U.S.

Number 21 to 30 Fastest Vanishing Jobs

21. Milling and planning machine setters, operators, and tenders, metal and plastic: -19.3% (job decline), $39,840 (median wage)

22. Forging machine setters, operators, and tenders, metal and plastic: -19.2% (job decline), $36,930 (median wage)

23. Legal secretaries: -19.1% (job decline), $44,180 (median wage)

24. Prepress technicians and workers: -19% (job decline), $38,930 (median wage)

25. Photographic process workers and processing machine operators: -18.4% (job decline), $26,470 (median wage)

26. Textile knitting and weaving machine setters, operators, and tenders: -18.3% (job decline), $27,470 (median wage)

27. Aircraft structure, surfaces, rigging, and systems assemblers: -17.4% (job decline), $50,050 (median wage)

28. Executive secretaries and executive administrative assistants: -17.4% (job decline), $55,860 (median wage)

29. Engine and other machine assemblers: -17.2% (job

decline), $41,210 (median wage)

30. Textile bleaching and dyeing machine operators and tenders: -17% (job decline), $27,270 (median wage)

In this tier, the 10 fast disappearing jobs are projected to decline anywhere from 19.3% and 17% between 2016 and 2026.

We see more manufacturing jobs here. In fact, 7 out of the 10 are machine operators, tenders, or assemblers.

Two of the 10 occupations are secretaries: Legal secretaries (#23) and executive secretaries and executive administrative assistants (#28). These are well paying jobs, but unfortunately they will not last.

Number 31 to 40 Fastest Vanishing Jobs

31. Postal service mail sorters, processors, and processing machine operators: -16.5% (job decline), $56,220 (median wage)

32. Textile winding, twisting, and drawing out machine setters, operators, and tenders: -16.3% (job decline), $27,500 (median wage)

33. Textile cutting machine setters, operators, and tenders: -15.8% (job decline), $26,090 (median wage)

34. Office machine operators, except computer: -15.6%

(job decline), $30,460 (median wage)

35. Patternmakers, metal and plastic: -15.5% (job decline), $44,210 (median wage)

36. Structural metal fabricators and fitters: -15.3% (job decline), $37,730 (median wage)

37. Extruding and drawing machine setters, operators, and tenders, metal and plastic: -15.2% (job decline), $33,870 (median wage)

38. Fabric and apparel patternmakers: -15% (job decline), $39,650 (median wage)

39. Molding, coremaking, and casting machine setters, operators, and tenders, metal and plastic: -15% (job decline), $30,480 (median wage)

40. Sewing machine operators: -14.2% (job decline), $23,670 (median wage)

In this tier, the 10 fast disappearing jobs are projected to decline anywhere from 16.5% and 14.2% between 2016 and 2026.

Most jobs in this tier are manufacturing related; we see a lot of jobs of machine operators, tenders, or assemblers.

Among the 10 disappearing jobs here, postal service mail sorters, processors, and processing machine operators (#31) are best paid at $56,220, followed by metal and plastic patternmakers (#35) at $44,210.

Number 41 to 50 Fastest Vanishing Jobs

41. Heat treating equipment setters, operators, and tenders, metal and plastic: -14.1% (job decline), $37,180 (median wage)

42. Desktop publishers: -13.9% (job decline), $41,090 (median wage)

43. Plating and coating machine setters, operators, and tenders, metal and plastic: -13.8% (job decline), $31,280 (median wage)

44. Assemblers and fabricators, all other: -13.8% (job decline), $28,550 (median wage)

45. Rolling machine setters, operators, and tenders, metal and plastic: -12.9% (job decline), $40,680 (median wage)

46. Team assemblers: -12.6% (job decline), $30,060 (median wage)

47. Coin, vending, and amusement machine servicers and repairers: -12.4% (job decline), $33,070 (median wage)

48. Model makers, metal and plastic: -12.2% (job decline), $48,550 (median wage)

49. Tire builders: -12.1% (job decline), $41,680 (median wage)

50. Postal service clerks: -12.1% (job decline), $56,790 (median wage)

In this tier, the 10 fast disappearing jobs are projected to decline anywhere from 14.1% and 12.1% between 2016 and 2026.

Manufacturing jobs continue to dominate here. In fact, 6 out of the 10 are machine operators, tenders, or assemblers.

Among the 10 disappearing jobs here, postal service clerks (#50) are best paid at $56,790, followed by metal and plastic model makers (#48) at $48,550.

Fast disappearing are also desktop publishers (#42) who are paid a good salary of $41,090, above the all-occupation median of $37,040.

Companies are expected to hire fewer desktop publishers as other types of workers—such as graphic designers, web designers, and editors—increasingly perform desktop-publishing tasks.

Number 51 to 60 Fastest Vanishing Jobs

51. Postal service mail carriers: -12.1% (job decline), $58,110 (median wage)

52. Print binding and finishing workers: -11.3% (job decline), $31,410 (median wage)

53. Radio and television announcers: -10.9% (job decline), $31,400 (median wage)

54. Reporters and correspondents: -10.7% (job decline), $37,820 (median wage)

55. Inspectors, testers, sorters, samplers, and weighers: -10.7% (job decline), $36,780 (median wage)

56. Fallers: -10.5% (job decline), $37,370 (median wage)

57. Welding, soldering, and brazing machine setters, operators, and tenders: -10.3% (job decline), $36,980 (median wage)

58. File clerks: -10.3% (job decline), $29,090 (median wage)

59. Nuclear power reactor operators: -10.2% (job decline), $91,170 (median wage)

60. Cutters and trimmers, hand: -10% (job decline), $27,600 (median wage)

In this tier, the 10 fast disappearing jobs are projected to decline anywhere from 12.1% and 10% between 2016 and 2026.

Among the 10 jobs here, nuclear power reactor operators

are best paid at $97,170 but are projected to lose 10.2% of the jobs in this occupation.

Renewable energy and new technologies that are making low-carbon power more reliable are growing rapidly in the U.S. Renewables are so cheap in some parts of the country that they are undercutting the price of older sources of electricity including nuclear power.

The impact has been significant on the nuclear industry, and a growing number of unprofitable reactors are shutting down. As a result, very good paying jobs such as nuclear power reactor operators are projected to decline.

Number 61 to 70 Fastest Vanishing Jobs

61. Grinding, lapping, polishing, and buffing machine tool setters, operators, and tenders, metal and plastic: -10% (job decline), $32,890 (median wage)

62. Motion picture projectionists: -9.9% (job decline), $22,100 (median wage)

63. Logging workers, all other: -9.5% (job decline), $38,950 (median wage)

64. Printing press operators: -9.4% (job decline), $35,530 (median wage)

65. Chemical plant and system operators: -9.2% (job decline), $59,920 (median wage)

66. Travel agents: -9.1% (job decline), $36,460 (median wage)

67. Paper goods machine setters, operators, and tenders: -9% (job decline), $36,990 (median wage)

68. Manufactured building and mobile home installers: -8.8% (job decline), $29,810 (median wage)

69. Cutting, punching, and press machine setters, operators, and tenders, metal and plastic: -8.7% (job decline), $32,370 (median wage)

70. Shoe machine operators and tenders: -8.5% (job decline), $26,150 (median wage)

In this tier, the 10 fast disappearing jobs are projected to decline anywhere from 10% and 8.5% between 2016 and 2026.

Among the 10 jobs here, eight are paid below the all-occupation median salary of $37,040.

Number 71 to 80 Fastest Vanishing Jobs

71. Extruding and forming machine setters, operators, and tenders, synthetic and glass fibers: -8.5% (job decline), $34,240 (median wage)

72. Lathe and turning machine tool setters, operators, and tenders, metal and plastic: -8.4% (job decline),

$38,480 (median wage)

73. Photographers: -8.4% (job decline), $34,070 (median wage)

74. Tellers: -8.3% (job decline), $27,260 (median wage)

75. Metal-refining furnace operators and tenders: -8.1% (job decline), $41,040 (median wage)

76. First-line supervisors of correctional officers: -7.8% (job decline), $60,560 (median wage)

77. Labor relations specialists: -7.8% (job decline), $62,310 (median wage)

78. Correctional officers and jailers: -7.7% (job decline), $42,820 (median wage)

79. Fabric menders, except garment: -7.6% (job decline), $26,920 (median wage)

80. Telecommunications equipment installers and repairers, except line installers: -7.6% (job decline), $53,640 (median wage)

In this tier, these 10 fast disappearing jobs are projected to decline anywhere from 8.5% and 7.6% between 2016 and 2026.

Six out of 10 jobs here are paying more than the all-occupation median salary of $37,040, with First-line supervisors of correctional officers best paid at $60, 560.

It is interesting to note that photographers are projected to lose 8.4% of their jobs between 2016 and 2026. A lot of people would think that given the explosion of online media, there should be more needs for photographers. True. Online media is growing fast and more photos are needed. However, this is only one of the several forces shaping up the future for photographers.

Other forces include shrinking digital cameras prices and a growing interest in photography by amateurs which diminishes the need for professional photographers.

Another force is the now ubiquitous cell phones equipped with high quality cameras and powerful software that creates a wide variety of photographical effects. It is now easy for an amateur or an average consumer to produce photos that approach professional quality.

Number 81 to 90 Fastest Vanishing Jobs

81. Computer programmers: -7.6% (job decline), $79,840 (median wage)

82. Mail clerks and mail machine operators, except postal service: -7.5% (job decline), $29,160 (median wage)

83. Tool and die makers: -7.3% (job decline), $51,060 (median wage)

84. Logging equipment operators: -7% (job decline), $37,490 (median wage)

85. Layout workers, metal and plastic: -6.8% (job decline), $45,820 (median wage)

86. Crushing, grinding, and polishing machine setters, operators, and tenders: -6.7% (job decline), $34,390 (median wage)

87. Pressers, textile, garment, and related materials: -6.7% (job decline), $21,300 (median wage)

88. Metal workers and plastic workers, all other: -6.6% (job decline), $33,280 (median wage)

89. Secretaries and administrative assistants, except legal, medical, and executive: -6.5% (job decline), $34,820 (median wage)

90. Rock splitters, quarry: -6.3% (job decline), $34,020 (median wage)

In this tier, the 10 fast disappearing jobs are projected to decline anywhere from 7.6% and 6.3% between 2016 and 2026.

Six out of 10 jobs here are paying less than the all-occupation median salary of $37,040, with textile, garment, and related materials pressers are paid a salary of only $21,300. It does not look good, and it is going to be even worse with the projection of losing 6.7% of its jobs in the years to come.

Number 91 to 100 Fastest Vanishing Jobs

91. New accounts clerks: -6.2% (job decline), $34,990 (median wage)

92. Buyers and purchasing agents, farm products: -5.9% (job decline), $58,430 (median wage)

93. Floral designers: -5.9% (job decline), $25,850 (median wage)

94. Adult basic and secondary education and literacy teachers and instructors: -5.6% (job decline), $50,650 (median wage)

95. Purchasing agents, except wholesale, retail, and farm products: -5.6% (job decline), $63,300 (median wage)

96. Extruding, forming, pressing, and compacting machine setters, operators, and tenders: -5.4% (job decline), $32,510 (median wage)

97. Roof bolters, mining: -5.2% (job decline), $56,780 (median wage)

98. Insurance underwriters: -5.2% (job decline), $67,680 (median wage)

99. Cooks, fast food: -5.2% (job decline), $19,860 (median

wage)

100. Semiconductor processors: -5.1% (job decline), $35,660 (median wage)

In this tier, the 10 fast disappearing jobs are projected to decline anywhere from 6.2% and 5.1% between 2016 and 2026.

Among the 10 occupations here, half are paid below the all-occupation median of $37,040, while the other half above. Insurance underwriters are best paid at $67,680, followed by Purchasing agents at $63,330.

So here we go, the top 100 fastest disappearing American jobs.

When you are out in the market looking for a job, consult this list and definitely try your best to steer clear of the ones on this list.

If you already have a job, please do also go through the list, too. If your current job is on this list, you might want to prepare for plan B and start exploring possibilities of migrating into another line of work, more secure and with better pay.

8 PERSONALIZED JOB RANKING

We are our choices.

— *Jean-Paul Sartre*

What we are today is a result of the choices we made yesterday. By the same token, what we will be tomorrow hinges on the choices we make today.

Nobody else but only ourselves are responsible for our destiny that will unfold itself according to the choices we make, including career choices.

Now we have found out a lot of information about occupations in previous chapters, including best paying jobs, fastest growing ones, fastest disappearing ones, states and metropolitan areas that have not only abundant job opportunities but also low unemployment rates, and the impact of education levels on the quality of jobs we can land.

How do we combine all these facets of occupations in a way to help us easily compare career options that are available to us? How do we distill all these pieces of information into one single career decision?

This is the topic of this chapter.

In this chapter, we introduce a method to rank systematically occupation options, based on criteria that can be individualized to each of us. This method is straightforward and easy to implement.

Once we apply the method to the job options we have, we will have a list of the job options ranked from best to worst, according to criteria that we care most in our individual circumstances.

This method incorporates the information we learned about occupations in this book. In addition, recall that in Chapter 1, we talked about not to make the choice of occupation solely based on wage and future demand of the profession.

The reader should also consider other critical aspects of going into a profession. For instance, is your heart truly in a particular line of work? Or do you hate doing things required by the job?

If you love an occupation from the bottom of your heart,

have a genuine interest in a job, or dream of having that job when growing up, you are highly likely to do well in that job because you will likely to stay focused and give out your best on the job.

Conversely, if you go for a job simply because it pays well, but in reality you actually hate the job, then you are highly likely to fail and find the job torturous.

Recall we typically spend at least 8 hours out of our waking hours on a job, plus commute time. If we hate what we do during the 8 hours on the job, every day from Monday to Friday, it will for sure reveal its grueling nature to us quickly.

Or you might be neutral in the job, not hugely passionate about it, nor do you hate it. In that case, it makes sense that the decision to join the profession can be heavily influenced by the big checks that the job brings home.

Hence, it is clear that our interest in a job is a critical aspect that must be included in our consideration.

In addition, we should identify the skill sets and education credentials required for getting into an occupation. Are you able to acquire the skill sets? Are you able to go and get that degree, financially and intellectually?

For example, rocket scientists sound cool and are paid well. But if you have trouble getting A's in high school math classes, it is better not to try to be a rocket scientist, but instead save the time, effort and money to work on something more attainable.

Furthermore, consider the investment of money, time and effort that you have to make before you can land a particular job.

As an example, we all know that medical doctors make a lot of money and do not seem to have trouble finding a job. However, becoming a doctor requires going through tough medical school years which are typically very expensive.

Although becoming a physician can lead to a very rewarding career, this level investment of money and time, together with the sacrifice of personal life, might not be the right choice for some of us.

So far, we have identified 6 factors that we had better include in our consideration when choosing an occupation, as follows:

1. Interest in the Job

2. Aptitude for the Job

3. Investment Affordability

4. Expected Wage

5. Future Demand for the Job

6. Job Location.

Let us now work out a way to combine these six factors into one single rank, for a given job. With a rank for a job, we can then easily make a decision based on the ranks of candidate occupations under our consideration.

The method is personalized, and reflects our own preferences toward occupations. Once we master it, this method will produce rankings of our candidate jobs better than any of the rankings you can find somewhere else.

The ranking produced here will suit our unique circumstances, while the people making those rankings elsewhere do not even know us. We know ourselves better than anyone else, and we are better suited than anyone else to make sound decisions for ourselves.

Let us walk through together this method below, step by step.

Step 1: Decide Relevant Factors

First, we need to ask ourselves this question: What are the aspects of an occupation that we truly care about?

There are no right or wrong answers to this question. But it does require us to look inward to our hearts: What do we really care about a job? What would make us happy about a job? What would make us unhappy?

It is recommended in this book to include at least the 6 factors mentioned above which are copied and pasted below again:

1.   Interest in the Job

2.   Aptitude for the Job

3.   Investment Affordability

4.   Expected Wage

5.   Future Demand for the Job

6.   Job Location.

If, after self-reflection, there are additional aspects of an occupation that we would like to incorporate into our consideration, add them to the list above.

In the remainder of this chapter, for the purpose of illustrating the ranking method, let us assume that we are content to settle with these 6 factors.

Step 2: Assign Weights to Factors

Next, we need to ask ourselves this question: How important to us are these six factors? Our answers to this question is incorporated into the ranking through assigning to the factors the weights of importance.

The way to go about assigning the weights is to pretend that you have 100 points and decide the way to allocate the 100 points to all the 6 factors according to the importance of the factors. The higher the weight, the more important is a factor.

For example, here is an example set of weights assigned to the factors:

1. Interest in the Job: weight 25

2. Aptitude for the Job: weight 15

3. Investment Affordability: weight 15

4. Expected Wage: weight 15

5. Future Demand: weight 15

6. Job Location: weight 15.

In this example, we are saying that five out of the six factors are equally important to us except for the 1st factor of Interest in the Job which is more important than the rest five.

Remember the weights have to sum up to 100, regardless how the 100 points are distributed across factors.

This allocation of 100 points forces us to think through and then decide the relative importance of the factors, according to our own priorities. Each of us might have different priorities, and therefore we might not agree with one another the relative importance of the factors, resulting in different allocations of the 100 points between us.

But this is exactly what we want. We want a ranking method that is personalized to our unique circumstance and our unique prioritization of the factors.

Keep in mind that the weights have to sum up to 100. If a factor appears more important than what we initially thought, additional points can be added to the weights of the factor, but these additional points must be taken from the weights of other factors.

Conversely, if we would like to reduce the weights of a specific factor, these points of reduction must be added to the weights of other factors so that the total sum of the weights remain 100.

Here is another example of the allocation of the 100 points:

1. Interest in the Job: weight 5

2. Aptitude for the Job: weight 5

3. Investment Affordability: weight 5

4. Expected Wage: weight 50

5. Future Demand: weight 30

6. Job Location: weight 5.

Here, on #1 Interest in the Job, we assign a tiny weight of 5 (out of the total 100 points), meaning that we are indifferent, neither passionate nor unpassionate, to what kind of occupations to take, compared with the importance of other factors to us. Therefore, only 5 points are allocated to allow it a small influence on our ranking.

On #2 Aptitude for the Job, we assign a miniscule weight of 5 (out of the total 100 points), signifying that we are confident that we are smart and have the adequate aptitude (or can acquire the aptitude) for any jobs we are interested in. Therefore, we are not concerned about #2 Aptitude. As a result, we assign #2 Aptitude a small weight of 5, meaning this has a small influence in the final ranking.

On #3 Investment Affordability, we assign also a trivial weight of 5 (out of the total 100 points), as we are determined to invest whatever it takes, in order to get the job. For example, we are willing to spend years to get the required education and are willing to take a loan to pay the tuition. Since we are so determined, we assign a small weight of 5 and let it have only a small influence on the ranking.

On #4 Expected Wage, we assign a heavy weight of 50, to indicate that the salary a job pays is the most important factor to us. Taking 50 points out of 100, this factor weighs as much as the combined importance of all the other five factors, allowing it to have a huge influence on the final ranking. In this case, we are certainly shooting for good money.

On #5 Future Demand, we assign a sizeable weight of 30, the second largest weight after #4 Expected Wage and much larger than the rest four factors. Great future demand guarantees a bright job growth outlook. Allocating a weight of 30 to this factor reflects our priority of looking for a job with a promising future over the other four factors (but lower than the salary the job would pay).

On #6 Job Location, we assign an insignificant weight of 5 (out of the total 100 points), to indicate that we are very willing to relocate, provided that the job satisfies us regarding other factors, particularly #4 Expected Wage and #5 Future Demand. This tiny weight of 5 allows only a small influence on the final ranking of candidate occupations under our consideration.

Hopefully the above two examples explicated the weight assignment for the six factors and the reasons for such an assignment.

So now let us think through the priorities of these six factors, decide the importance of them, and design a set of weights that best reflect our priorities among the factors.

Once we have assigned the weights, we stick to them and use them across all candidate jobs.

Now that we have completed Step 2, let us proceed to the next step.

Step 3: Score Each Factor

Scoring each factor means assigning a number to a factor to reflect the degree of satisfaction that a given job gives us with respect to the factor.

The example below will help us understand what scoring is. We need to note that a good portion of this scoring is subjective, particularly for #1 Interest in the Job, #2 Aptitude for the Job, #3 Investment Affordability, and #6 Job Location.

But we can use the wage and job growth outlook information we learned in previous chapters to inform us in scoring #4 Expected Wage and #5 Future Demand.

Let us decide that the scale of the score is 1 to 10, with 1 being most unsatisfying and 10 most satisfying. For each factor, we will assign a number within this range.

Note that the scoring scale is arbitrary so long as the scale provides sufficient differentiation. We picked the scale of 1 to 10 for convenience and also for the fact that the range of 1 to 10 is granular enough for this example.

To illustrate the scoring process, let us use an example occupation of pharmacists.

Here is my scoring on the six factors for the pharmacist occupation. The scores work together with the weights we just discussed above. Therefore, in this scoring example, along the scores, the factor weights used in the last example above are also shown below.

It needs to be stressed that the scores below are made up for illustration purposes only. When you do your own scoring, make sure the score reflects your choice on the scale of 1 to 10.

1. Interest in the Job: weight 5, score 6

    The score assign to this factor should reflect our interest in the job which is pharmacists in this example. I am not particularly interested in pharmacy, but I do not despise it, either. I can devote to the job if needed. Therefore, I give it a neutral score of 6, very close to the midpoint of the scale of 1 to 10.

    If this job interested me very much, I would have assigned a high score of 8, 9, or even the perfect 10.

2. Aptitude for the Job: weight 5, score 8

    The score assign to this factor should reflect our ability to do the job well that either exists or is easy to acquire through education and training. To excel as a pharmacist, we need good memory to take all those drug names, disease names, and prescriptions into our brain. I feel that I have pretty good memory and that I will likely do well in memorizing all these. Hence, I give it a strong score of 4, as I am equipped with the required aptitude.

If I felt not confident about my memory, I would have assigned a low score to this factor to indicate that I potentially lack the ability to do well on the job.

3. Investment Affordability: weight 5, score 10

    After some research, I learned that to become a pharmacist, I will have to first complete two years of undergraduate course work, and then pass the Pharmacy College Admission Test (PCAT). I will then begin a four-year pharmacy program to obtain a doctorate of Pharmacy degree. After the degree, there will be a 1- to 2-year residency requirement. So, in total, I am looking at six years in school, plus up to two years of residency.

    I am prepared to invest this much of time, and the associated the tuition and other costs of going through the six school years. Since I am highly motivated to make such investment, I assign the highest score of 10 to this factor.

    If I felt that such investment is way over my head, I would have assigned a low score.

4. Expected Wage: weight 50, score 8

    In the wage data released by the U.S. Department of Labor in 2017, an average pharmacist takes home $122,230, #24 in the 100 highest paying jobs. Not bad at all. Although in previous chapters, we saw that there are occupations where an average worker earns $200,000+, what an average pharmacist makes is already pretty good to me. I, therefore, assign a strong score of 8 to this factor.

If I aimed really high, say, above $200,000, the salary of $122,230 would not have satisfied much. As a result, I would have assigned here a low score.

5. Future Demand: weight 30, score 4.

   After research, on the one hand, I found out that between 2016 and 2026, the occupation of pharmacists is projected to grow 5.6%, slower than the average growth of 7.4% across all occupations.

   On the other hand, it is growing but not declining, unlike some sunset occupations. Therefore, assigning a low score of 2 to the Future Demand factor feels appropriate to me.

6. Job Location: weight 5, score 9.

   It is clear that the pharmacist job is needed everywhere across the country, without any particularly unusual geographical concentration.

   In addition, after research, I found out that the top 5 states that employ the most pharmacists are California, Texas, Florida, New York, and Pennsylvania. I would be happy to relocate to any of these places.

Given that the location of pharmacist jobs is not restrictive at all, I assign it a high score of 9.

Just as an example, if hypothetically, Chicago was a hub of the pharmacist jobs, and I know I hated the long, cold, and windy weather in Chicago winters, I would have assigned a very low score of 1 here.

With each factor already scored, we can now move on to the next step.

Step 4: Calculate the Total Score

In this step, we multiply the weight by the score to obtain the weighted score, for each factor, as follows:

1. Interest in the Job: weight 5 × score 6 = 30

2. Aptitude for the Job: weight 5 × score 8 = 40

3. Investment Affordability: weight 5 × score 10 = 50

4. Expected Wage: weight 50 × score 8 = 400

5. Future Demand: weight 30 × score 4 = 120

6. Job Location: weight 5 × score 9 = 45.

Summing weighted scores over factors, we have 30 + 40 + 50 + 400 + 120 + 45 = 685. Our *total weighted score* for the occupation of pharmacists is 685.

We note that the perfect score for each factor scores is 10. Because we have total weights of 100 points spread across all the six factors, the *perfect total weighted score* is 10 × 100 = 1,000. This perfect total weighted score happens when each of the six factor scores a perfect 10.

Dividing the total weighted score 685 for pharmacists by the perfect total weighted score of 1,000 gives the *final score* of 68.5%, certainly above the average but not close to a perfect job which would have scored 100%. The final score of 68.5% can be used for ranking candidate occupations.

Therefore, in four easy steps, we now have a ranking for the occupation of pharmacists, taking into account six factors that we care about in making career decisions.

Another Example

Let us consider another candidate occupation that we are comparing with the pharmacist occupation. This other candidate occupation is application software developers which has a median wage of $100,080, lower than that of pharmacist of $122,230. Over the period of 2016 to 2026, application software developers are projected to grow an amazing 30.5%, much faster than the growth of 5.6% for pharmacist jobs.

In addition, I know that programming is where my

passion lies, and in particular, I am highly interested in developing application software. Moreover, I excel at logical thinking and thus have excellent aptitude for the programmer job.

To become an application software developer, I need only an undergraduate degree, preferably in the computer science major. This will take only four years, an investment that is well affordable to me.

With these pieces of information and self-assessment, here is the scoring for the factors:

1. Interest in the Job: weight 5 × score 10 = 50

2. Aptitude for the Job: weight 5 × score 10 = 50

3. Investment Affordability: weight 5 × score 10 = 50

4. Expected Wage: weight 50 × score 7 = 350

5. Future Demand: weight 30 × score 9 = 270

6. Job Location: weight 5 × score 10 = 50.

Note that the factor weights are kept the same as in the pharmacist example, but the factor scores change, when comparing different occupations.

Summing over all the six factors give us the total weighted score of 50 + 50 + 50 + 350 + 270 + 50 = 820. Dividing 820 by the perfect total weighted score of 1,000 gives us 82%.

This is much better than 68.5% we had before for the pharmacist job.

Comparing the final score of 82% for application software developers with that of 68.5% for pharmacists, we would choose to become an application software developer over a pharmacist.

Although pharmacists take home a median salary of $122,230, much higher than that of application software developers ($100,080), the pharmacists lose out to application software developers in every other factor, resulting in a lower final score.

We stress again this score is completely personalized to each individual of us, through our own choice of weights and scores for the factors. For the same occupation of pharmacists, another person might produce a completely different final score and thus different ranking among all candidate occupations.

Within the confines of the subjective choices of weights and scores, this ranking method provides a logical, consistent, and transparent way of comparing candidate occupations.

If we are on the fence between several choices, with each one having its own pros and cons, this method helps us crystalize our own thoughts, rationalize our priorities, and make a sound decision that brings peace to our mind.

There are situations where we are very clear about what occupation to go into. For example, some of us always dream of becoming a school teacher when growing up, and nothing will change our mind.

Even in these cases, this method can help us discover the tradeoffs of taking the teachers occupation versus other choices, and helps us ascend to a higher level of consciousness in terms of career choices, regardless of whether or not this would make us rethink about the teachers occupation.

So, pull out a piece of paper and a pencil, write down your candidate jobs, decide the weights of the factors, score each candidate job, and in the end, you will have a ranking of all these candidate jobs. This ranking will make your career decisions a lot easier and a lot better, at the same time.

9 ADDITIONAL INFORMATION

This book thus far has presented a wealth of information about America's best jobs, from a variety of angles. Unfortunately, due to limited space in the book, the majority of the 820 occupations in the United States did not have an opportunity to be shown here.

The reader, however, can find a complete list of the 820 occupations in the book titled *The Complete List of American Jobs*. In the book, every occupation is listed out with the following information:

- Median Salary

- Ninetieth Percentile Salary

- Project Growth Between 2016 and 2026

- Typical Education Needed for Entry Into the Occupation

Recall that the median salary of an occupation refers to the typical salary paid to secretaries. Or equivalently, by the median salary, we mean the salary paid to an average worker. See Chapter 2 for a more detailed explanation.

The 90th percentile salary is the salary that is better than 90% of the salaries paid to workers in an occupation. Thus, it serves as a measure of how much we can make if we excel at our jobs, beyond being an average worker.

The book is for the reader who would like to look up a particular occupation for its rank among the 820 occupations, regarding the information listed above.

This is it. For now. Thank you for reading this book.

As parting words, before we meet again in another book, the author sincerely wishes the reader best of luck in landing dream jobs.

For any questions, the author can be reached at jon.macon@outlook.com.

ABOUT THE AUTHOR

Jon Macon, Ph.D., author of two books titled America's Best Jobs and The Complete List of American Jobs, has a passion for writing about strategic career choices. Through writing, Jon advocates career planning based on insights distilled from massive employment data now afforded by technological advances. During the waking hours when Jon does not write, he heads up an analytics division at a tier 1 investment bank on Wall Street. Jon can be reached at Jon.Macon@outlook.com.

28703757R00126

Made in the USA
Columbia, SC
21 October 2018